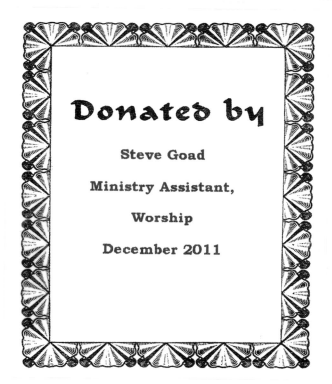

In Search
of Morality

Other books by Robert A. Schuller

Power to Grow beyond Yourself
Strength for the Fragile Spirit
Just Because You're on a Roll . . . Doesn't Mean
    You're Going Downhill
Dump Your Hang-Ups . . . without Dumping Them
    on Others
What Happens to Good People When Bad Things Happen

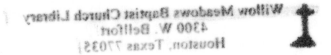

In Search of Morality

How You Can Live a Fulfilling Life from the Inside Out

Robert A. Schuller

Fleming H. Revell

A Division of Baker Book House Co
Grand Rapids, Michigan 49516

Published by Fleming H. Revell
a division of Baker Book House Company
P.O. Box 6287, Grand Rapids, MI 49516-6287

Printed in the United States of America

Library of Congress Cataloging-in-Publication Data

Schuller, Robert A.
    In search of morality : how you can live a fulfilling life from the inside out / Robert A. Schuller.
      p.   cm.
    Includes bibliographical references.
    ISBN 0-8007-1735-X
      1. Christian ethics. 2. United States—Moral conditions. I. Title.
BJ1251.S29   1997
241—dc21
                                    96-38086

Unless otherwise indicated, Scripture quotations are taken from the HOLY BIBLE, NEW INTERNATIONAL VERSION®. NIV®. Copyright ©1973, 1978, 1984 by International Bible Society. Used by permission of Zondervan Publishing House. All rights reserved.

Scripture from THE MESSAGE. Copyright © by Eugene H. Peterson 1993, 1994, 1995. Used by permission of NavPress Publishing Group.

For current information about all releases from Baker Book House, visit our web site: http://www.bakerbooks.com

Illustrations on p. 46 copyright by Bill Bright, New Life Publications, Orlando, FL 32859-3684. Used by permission.

"The Road Not Taken" on p. 68 is reprinted by permission of Henry Holt and Company, Inc., New York, NY 10011.

Contents

Preface

Ruby Bridges did the right thing.

It happened in New Orleans, forty years ago.

Ruby Bridges was six years old—a little girl standing strong in the middle of a storm of angry emotions that was not of her own making. It was a storm that was not precipitated by anything she had done or said, but merely by the color of her skin.

Ruby Bridges was black. The storm that raged around her was due to a federal judge's ruling that she be allowed to attend school with white children.

Although Ruby Bridges didn't know it, she was striking a blow to the heart of a monster called segregation. And monsters never die easily.

It seemed that everyone in New Orleans was scared. White parents were scared because they didn't want their children to go to school with black children. Black parents were scared because they were afraid their children would be hurt if they tried to send them to the white schools. So all the children stayed home.

All, that is, except for Ruby Bridges.

She was there right on time when the morning school bell rang. With two federal agents in front of her and two more behind her, she walked through the crowd that ridiculed and insulted her. With her head held high, she broke through the barrier that had divided this country for so long. As her last name implies, she began to build bridges between blacks and whites not only in New Orleans but also throughout the United States.

I have seen photos of that little girl bravely confronting the angry mob that would have done just about anything to keep her out of "their" schools—and I wonder: would I have been strong enough to do what Ruby Bridges did? What about you? How did a little girl find that kind of strength?

It takes a tremendous amount of strength to do what is right in a world that often seems to take delight in what is obviously wrong. It takes strength to face the "monsters" of our world head-on, to look them in the eye without flinching and say, "I'm not going to give in."

For just as there was evil and injustice in the world Ruby Bridges faced when she was a little girl, there is evil and injustice in the world we all face today. May God grant us the courage to face the storms that confront us just as Ruby Bridges confronted the storm that raged against her all those years ago.

PART 1

Do the Right Thing

1

Assume Moral Responsibility

One of the greatest delusions in the world is the hope that
the evils in this world are to be cured by legislation.

Thomas B. Reed

Look around and you'll see that the society in which we
live increasingly seems to be missing something very important, something called morality.

Sadly, the absence of morality carries with it a terrible price
tag. Broken homes. Broken hearts. Broken people. Lost ideals.
Lost hopes. Lost dreams. Damaged relationships and damaged people. People in pain who thought they could slide
through life doing whatever they wanted to do are now dis-
covering the cost attached to the living of an amoral life.

Things in America are not at all what they ought to be. These
words from former Secretary of Education William J. Bennett
are sobering:

A few months ago I had lunch with a friend of mine, a man who
has written for a number of political journals and who now lives in

11

Asia. During our conversation, the topic turned to America—specifically, America as seen through the eyes of foreigners.

During our conversation, he told me what he had observed during his travels: that while the world still regards the United States as the leading economic and military power on earth, this same world no longer beholds us with the moral respect it once did. When the rest of the world looks at America, he said, they see no longer a "shining city on a hill." Instead, they see a society in decline, with exploding rates of crime and social pathologies. We all know that foreigners often come here in fear—and once they are here, they travel in fear. It is to our shame to realize that they have good reason to fear; a record number of them get killed here.

Today, many who come to America believe they are visiting a degraded society.[1]

Is that true? Are they visiting a "degraded society," and if they are, then what has happened here in America?

Think for a moment about the changes that have taken place in our society over the last few generations.

For example, there was a tremendous uproar back in the 1930s when Clark Gable uttered the four-letter word *damn* in *Gone with the Wind*. People could not believe that such profanity had been allowed on the movie screen.

Have you been to the theater lately? It's very difficult to find a movie that's not peppered with the worst sort of language—language that a few years ago wouldn't have been uttered by a group of the crassest of men. And now theaters full of teenagers and children are being subjected to unbelievable filth, all in the name of "reality."

Not long ago I was waiting in line to get into a movie and I couldn't help but overhear the conversation taking place in front of me between two teenage girls. They were using language that would cause a Marine to blush. I was embarrassed for them but then I figured that because they've heard people talk that way in the movies they probably think it's normal—an accepted part of ordinary conversation.

Some may say, "Oh, come on, it's only words." But the words we use are an important indication of who we are as a people. Language that is cheap, shallow, and laced with obscenity is a reflection of cheap, shallow, and obscene lives.

Of course, as anyone knows, language isn't the only problem with today's movies. They are also full of sex, violence, and perversions of all sort. This cannot be helpful in a society dealing with soaring rates of crime and sexually transmitted disease.

Then there is today's music. I have heard that when Elvis Presley made his first appearance on the *Ed Sullivan Show*, cameramen were instructed to show Presley from the waist up. Sullivan felt that Presley's swiveling hips bordered on obscene and he did not want to be responsible for broadcasting them into the living rooms of millions of American families. But have you seen a music video lately? Have you listened to a "gangsta rap"? Do you remember what happened to rapper Tupac Shakur? He was gunned down in the streets of Vegas—an event that mirrored the lyrics and beat of his work.

Violence. Perverted sex. Murder. Hatred and disrespect for women. Racial hatred. To a great degree, these are the themes of today's popular music.

Yes, something is terribly wrong in our society.

As James A. Baker III writes:

According to a recent poll, 73 percent of Americans worry that the nation is experiencing a moral decline. They are right to be concerned.

The symptoms of America's social decay hardly bear repeating. The explosive rise of illegitimacy since 1960 has plunged millions into material poverty and moral dependence. An epidemic of crime has created a climate of fear in many neighborhoods and schools.

Much of our popular culture is dominated by promiscuity, violence—or both. Worse yet, our judicial and educational systems often seem helpless to stem the rising tide of social decay.[2]

How did this happen to our society? I believe that it began almost imperceptibly, with minor changes, which in turn brought about other, greater changes. The overall effect was not unlike an avalanche, started by a few small pebbles tumbling downhill.

For example, I can think of one change that might be regarded by most as insignificant but that nonetheless has had an important impact on our society.

When I was a small boy, many stores were closed on Sunday because that was "the Lord's Day." In many areas of the United States, their closure was mandated by blue laws. Over time, blue laws began to be overturned, and now Sunday is just another day of buying and trading, indistinguishable from any other day of the week.

This provides more time for people to shop and puts extra dollars in the pockets of merchants. But there has been a high price to pay. We have lost the sanctity of Sunday, the one day of the week when most American families could be together and when time was set aside to honor God. I understand that we don't all set aside Sunday as a holy day—not even all Christians do this. But there was something vital to the moral strength of our nation in our setting aside a day when most families could be together.

I'm not saying that the repealing of blue laws has caused our society to slip into moral decay. We need to be responsible citizens, doing what we know is right, and not depend on society to dictate it to us. All I am saying is that it is a sign and symptom of what is going on elsewhere in society. It is a reflection of the way things have changed in America over the last 150 years.

In 1850 the underlying ethic in America was the Protestant work ethic. In 1900, with the influx of Catholic immigrants, it was the Christian ethic. In the 1950s we began to speak of the Judeo-Christian ethic. And then, as the revolution of the sixties opened our society up to Eastern mysticism, we began to think in terms of a monotheistic ethic. Slowly the spiritual ethic began to give way to individualism and secular humanism. Do what you want, whenever you want, however you want.

Writing in *Christianity Today*, Charles Colson and Jack Eckerd say:

> Americans have largely forgotten the place of thrift, industry, diligence and perseverance—ideals summed up by the words *work ethic*. From the sturdy Scottish Protestants to the Italian Catholics and enterprising Jewish immigrants, from the tiny country churches to the synagogues to the grand cathedrals of the cities, America was built by a religious people. And one of the basic beliefs they brought with them was that, in the words of writer Arthur Burns, "their work mattered to God."
>
> Set within us from the beginning, this purposeful nature drives us to work hard, to be productive, to create, and to accumulate the results of our labor. Work is thus a moral imperative.[3]

If you want more evidence that something is wrong in our society, just take a look at what is happening in our schools.

William J. Bennett says that in 1940 when teachers were asked to identify the top problems in America's schools, they listed talking out of turn, chewing gum, making noise, running in the hall, cutting in line, dress code infractions, and littering. But when teachers in 1990 were asked the same question they said the top problems were drug use, alcohol abuse, pregnancy, suicide, rape, robbery, and assault.[4]

That quick look at how far we have fallen sends a chill racing down my backbone.

Bennett also cites figures showing that in the thirty years between 1960 and 1990

> there has been a 560 percent increase in violent crime; more than a 400 percent increase in illegitimate births; a quadrupling in divorces; a tripling of the percentage of children living in single-parent homes; more than a 200 percent increase in the teenage suicide rate and a drop of 75 points in the average S.A.T. scores of high-school students.[5]

Yes, It Really Is That Bad

You may be reading this and thinking, *Aren't you exaggerating?* No, I'm not. Things really are that bad in America today.

Anthony Harrigan, writing in the *St. Croix Review,* believes that our civilization is at stake:

> As a people, we have many national life-threatening problems of a mundane character. One thinks of the almost terminal disorder of our country's fiscal affairs, our citizens' inability to save and plan for the future, homelessness, the deterioration of our educational system, the existence of urban violence and drug-related crime. I believe, however, given a restoration of values, that disorders can be overcome. But one should be deeply worried by the ills in our society that point to a fatal fragmentation of the society created in America since the early 1600s. What's at stake is our branch of Western civilization. Many thoughtful Americans are concerned about survival of the inner values of our civilization, the weakened standards of our civilization, under the conditions which exist today and which are likely to exist in the opening decades of the 21st century.[6]

Dwight D. Murphey, a business law professor at Wichita State University in Kansas, lists a number of ways in which he believes "internal barbarism" is on the rise in the United States.[7]

Violent crime. In 1991 the FBI released a study titled "Crime in the United States," which reported that violent crimes that year were up 5 percent over the previous year and had climbed by 45 percent since 1982. That report also stated that a growing number of youngsters between the ages of ten and seventeen were being arrested for crimes ranging from murder and rape to drug abuse and weapons violations.

Drugs. In early 1993 a federally funded survey conducted by the University of Michigan discovered that junior high school students are increasingly involved with drugs of all kinds, including marijuana, cocaine, LSD, and inhalants. Some 11.2 percent of the thirteen- and fourteen-year-olds surveyed said they had tried marijuana.

Sexually transmitted diseases. It is reported that three million American teenagers contract sexually transmitted diseases every year. Syphilis is at its highest level in forty years, with 134,000 new cases reported every year. What's more, 1.3 million new cases of gonorrhea are reported annually. It is estimated that as many as one million Americans carry the AIDS virus and more than three hundred thousand in this country have died from the disease.

Children born out of wedlock. More than a million babies are born out of wedlock in America every year. Murphey points out that there is a strong connection between such births and low birth weight, high infant mortality, and poverty. Murphey says:

> There is a direct correlation between unmarried parentage and poverty. An article by Robert Rector in the *Washington Times* in September 1992 told how "the poverty rate for married-couple families was just 5.6 percent [in 1990]. For married couples with a full-time worker it was just 2 percent. By contrast, the poverty rate of female-headed families was a staggering 32.2 percent."

Loss of integrity. Murphey writes:

> A February 2, 1992, report in the *Wichita Eagle* observed that "critics say fraud has been an important force in pushing up the premiums Americans have to pay for auto insurance, from $40 billion to $100 billion since 1980." The article points to "fraudulent claims—everything from reporting accidents that never happened, to exaggerated car damage to faked injuries.... In Massachusetts, the insurance industry has long estimated fraud at 10 percent of auto claims filed. On Long Island, N.Y., Nassau County police have concluded that 50 percent to 60 percent of the hundreds of people who report their cars stolen from the Green Acres shopping mall . . . have actually abandoned or destroyed them for the insurance money."
>
> The honest American stands, in effect, like a giant oak covered by parasitical, life-sucking vines. Add up the fraud, the passed-along costs such as the medical bills, the enormous volume of shoplifting and the equally voluminous employee theft, and what do we have?—a vast incubus on the backs of productive people.
>
> It is imperative that we reaffirm our commitment to a free society and to civilization. The barbarism must not be allowed to define our existence, even as we combat it. For example, our recourse must be to law, not to the vigilantism that will inevitably grow if lawful measures aren't taken; to an increased demand for what is truly valuable in art and music, films and literature, not to censorship. Otherwise, the barbarism will have struck its worst blow without our own souls.

Those are some of the problems. But what do we do about them?

Passing More Laws Is Not the Answer

Some people are quick to say that we need more and tougher laws to keep the "dangerous elements" of our society in check.

But what's going on here is that we are all falling prey to the changing mores of society. Sometimes it's hard to know the difference between right and wrong. But just because everyone else is doing something doesn't make it right. Nor can we say that this or that action is morally right simply because it is "supported" by our country's laws. The truth is that many of our laws are immoral.

A hundred years ago we could use the ethos of society and the law as a crutch to undergird what was right and wrong. First century Christians in Rome, Corinth, or Ephesus didn't have such a crutch. Nor do Christians today in Bombay, Cairo, or Copenhagen. Nor do we. How then do we make our ethical and moral decisions? How do we teach our kids to make right decisions?

We say, "There ought to be a law," but increasingly, laws are opening the doors to all kinds of behavior that the Bible decries. We can no longer depend on laws—even in matters like euthanasia or genetic planning.

Yes, we ought to be angry and we ought to want to do something to stop the slide into moral decay . . . and pain.

But what can we do? How can we do it? Where can we go for the answers and the strength we need to rediscover our moral strength as individuals and as a nation?

We must allow the Spirit of God to work within us and penetrate every fiber. We must take personal responsibility for allowing the Holy Spirit to show us where change is needed. We cannot change others. Only God can do that. We can change ourselves and we will change for the better as we accept the gifts of God.

2

Morality Comes from Inside Out

So I say, live by the Spirit, and you will not gratify the desires of the sinful nature. . . . They are in conflict with each other, so that you do not do what you want. But if you are led by the Spirit, you are not under law.

Galatians 5:16–18

In America today many people are trying to construct the moral fabric of their lives out of our various laws and legal codes. Some people feel they have the right to do anything as long as it is not expressly forbidden by the law, but they're wrong.

There is an old saying that goes like this: "In England you can go anywhere as long as you are dressed correctly. In France you can say anything as long as you say it correctly. In America you can do anything as long as you make a profit."

That's one theory of morality, and sadly enough, it's a theory that some people live by. It's a faulty theory to be sure, and dangerous. I call people who live this way "legal moralists." They believe that the law is our moral code. If something is legal, then it follows that it must be moral, no matter what it is. Abortion can be used as a means of contraception. Any form of profiteering is fine as long as there is a loophole in the law that allows it. There are no boundaries. Sexuality becomes hedonistic.

You see, our legal system is not based on morality—at all. It has historically been justified as a reflection of our morality as a nation but it is not really based on morality.

There are others in our society who are calling for obedience to a different type of morality. These are the people I call "moral legalists." They believe that our morals must shape our law. They are the ones the media calls "right-wing Christian fundamentalists." They are the ones who know, beyond any doubt, what is right and wrong and they want to see their own moral code become the law of the land.

I cannot agree.

If morality is used as the basis for our country's legal code, I believe this would create a system that would destroy the freedom we Americans value so highly. If you want to know what life is like in a country that has a moral basis for its laws, just take a look at Iran and Saudi Arabia. I do not want to live in either one of those countries, thank you very much.

I have a friend who is a flight attendant on corporate jets. On several occasions she has flown oil executives to Saudi Arabia. I asked her if it is as restrictive in that country as I have been led to believe. She said, "It's terrible. I have to have every area of my body covered at all times. If part of my arm happens to be showing, I'm told to cover myself up or else they will call the police and have me arrested."

Is it preposterous to think that such a thing could happen here? All I can say is that I do not want anyone else, no matter how sincere or "spiritual" he or she might be, deciding for me how I must think and act in matters of personal morality.

I am an ordained minister in the Reformed Church in America. This denomination can trace its roots all the way back to the Reformation of the sixteenth century. It was the fathers of this church who bought a small island named Manhattan in the early 1600s. In fact the Reformed Church is the oldest corporation in America. These leaders of my denomination came to America from the Netherlands in search of religious freedom. In Europe they were being persecuted for their stand against the church of Rome. Here they would receive their freedom to worship and live as they saw fit.

I find it threatening that some people would take this freedom from me in the name of morality. They want to create a legal system based on their interpretation of the Bible, and I don't trust all of their interpretations. Therefore, I want our judicial system to be based on human rights and the freedom of all. Anything short of this will limit my freedom to worship God the way I want to.

It is impossible to create a moral code that all people must fit into. When I first planned this book, I thought I would be writing such a moral code. I thought I would be able to decipher what was right and wrong and communicate it to the masses. I was going to tell the truth in such a way that all those who read this book would begin living fuller and happier lives. But as my studies into the subject unfolded, I discovered to my surprise that it is not possible to dictate morality. Only God can say what is right or wrong in every instance.

Please understand that I am talking about issues that are not clearly addressed in the Bible, such topics as abortion, genetic engineering, artificial insemination, smoking, gambling, drugs, and dress. Of course, there are those acts that are clearly immoral. We can look at the Ten Commandments and other moral codes going all the way back to Hammurabi and realize that the same ethics continue to rise to the surface. The laws of every state include most of these codes: Thou shalt not kill; Thou shalt not steal; and so on.

What I am talking about here are those actions that fall into the gray areas. Some of today's most difficult moral issues aren't even addressed by the Bible. Like abortion, for instance. You can search the Bible all you want, looking for a Scripture that uses the word *abortion*, and you won't find it. It's just not there. You can find the text in the Bible that says, "Do not kill," but that takes you right into the debate of when life begins. I don't want to address either argument here. I simply want to point out that there is a lack of clarity on issues such as this or there wouldn't be any arguments at all.

This is one of many areas where we must make personal decisions that are not based on the law of the land and that go beyond what the Bible prescribes for us.

Obviously many areas of moral behavior are addressed directly in the Bible. The most casual reader knows that killing, stealing, lying, and committing adultery are forbidden. But there are at least as many areas where the Bible is silent. Only when we are led by the Spirit of God can we make proper decisions regarding what is right and wrong in those areas. Only when we are led by the Spirit can we decide how we ought to behave in areas where there seems to be latitude scripturally. Only then can we live in such a way that our lives are pleasing to God.

Let me give you an example of something I run into often. Many of the couples who are married at Rancho Capistrano

Community Church began living together before they decided to "make it legal." They entered into a sexual relationship prior to marriage. Some did so with the understanding that they were going to get married. They made a commitment to each other before they entered into sexual relations, and then they formalized their commitment to each other through marriage.

This raises an interesting question: At what point does an unwed person enter into adultery? Does sex before marriage always constitute adultery? When is a "marriage" consummated? What about Adam and Eve? They did not have a church wedding! What constituted their marriage? Was it the sexual act itself or was there more to it?[1]

The Hebrew author states that they "knew" each other. The implication is that they not only had sex, but that they also had a relationship that was deeply spiritual. They had an understanding of each other that created a union that had meaning and gave them perpetuity.

I know some married couples who don't know each other and I know some couples who are living together without the benefit of marriage who know each other very well. Which of these couples do you think is married in the eyes of God? Is it possible that the couple that is married only in a legal sense, and that has a sexual relationship but no real love, is in God's eyes guilty of adultery?

It is very hard to talk about morality without becoming judgmental, despite Jesus' warnings against judging others. As for me, every time I'm tempted to judge someone for his or her behavior, I remember the words of John Bradford, who said, "There but for the grace of God go I." Every time I see a drunk on the street I am reminded of those words.

Morality Is a Personal Matter

The search for morality is a search for personal responsibility. I believe that true morality looks only at self and does not look at everyone else. It does not impose its code on others. True morality comes from the inside out and not from the outside in.

Morality from the inside out is what the apostle Paul is talking about in his letter to the Galatians. That is why part 2 of this book discusses the fruit of the Spirit listed in Galatians 5:22. I have read many commentaries and books on those nine fruit. Not one of those commentaries or books recognized the connection of the nine fruit to personal morality. Nor did they incorporate the need to be free from the law in order to live by the Spirit. I believe they have missed something of vital importance.

To experience the fruit of the Spirit in your life is to come to a place of peace and contentment, to live a life of personal morality that is pleasing to yourself and, most important, to God.

Morality from the inside out allows the gifts of the Spirit to grow from within and produces a positive, healthy, and whole person. The person who exhibits these fruit in his or her life sees the tremendous grace of God everywhere. He or she knows that God's mercies abound.

It reminds me of the testimony of one of our new members at the Crystal Cathedral, Freddy Topete. When he joined the church at the age of twenty-four, he had already had twenty-five operations with more to come. It started when he was twelve.

"I was very wild. I began deceiving my parents. I started smoking marijuana and got involved in a gang of older kids. By the age of sixteen I had tried everything and thought I had it all. Then the accident. It was September 24, 1989. I had been in a gang fight. I took off on my motorcycle and ran into a parked bus. When I awoke I was in the hospital, nearly dead. I had sustained massive injuries to my esophagus, lungs, liver, stomach, and kidneys. My arms and legs were broken. I could not move or speak. I was in the hospital for fourteen months.

"During one of my physical therapy sessions at the hospital, I happened to look out the window where I saw the reflection of a cross. I felt as though God had his arms opened and was speaking directly to me telling me, 'Freddy I love you.' I felt peace and serenity come over me. Jesus loved me and had forgiven me!

"I told my mother that I wanted to go to the church with the cross. She told me that the church was only for Anglos. But then she discovered that there is a Hispanic ministry at Crystal Cathedral. She brought me here and now this is my church.

"I was told that I would never walk, talk, or eat through my mouth. The doctors gave up on me. But today, thanks to God, I can do all those things because of the new faith I have found. I will always remember the cross reflected through the window and his arms opened wide just for me."

In contrast to morality from the inside out, there is morality from the outside in. This form of morality creates a code of ethics to live by. It tries to live under the law and measures its success by whether or not it fulfilled its laws for the day. Follow this line of thinking and you are free from responsibility. There is no need to be proactive in reaching out to help others. After all, there is no law that compels you to do this.

It is when you go beyond that type of thinking and begin actively trying to make this world a better place that you enter the internal working of God on human flesh.

The Immoral Miss All the Fun

I sometimes ask myself why some people make a conscious decision not to live a moral life. I have heard people say, "I don't want to miss the fun." But I believe that those who truly "miss the fun" are those who refuse to live according to God's laws. I believe in the Bible and that an understanding of God's laws is crucial for anyone who wants to get the most out of life. Because God created the world, he surely knows how it works. That is why I often refer to the Bible as "the manufacturer's handbook." Anyone who ignores it does so at his or her own risk.

I have used this illustration many times, but I want to share it with you again. I was in Israel, leading a group of about thirty people in the footsteps of Jesus. My group had checked into a brand-new hotel that probably should not have been open. It was still being built and some of the rooms weren't yet finished. When I went to my room, I was delighted to see that my pillows had never been used. I took the plastic off myself. Then I went out to the balcony because I wanted to check out the view.

That was when I realized they hadn't quite finished everything. The rail around the balcony had not been installed. Here I was on the fourteenth floor with what looked like a diving platform outside. They had put a dowel in the sliding door to keep guests from going out but that didn't stop me. I pulled that stop out of the track, opened the door, and very carefully ventured out onto the platform. I stood in the center and took a quick look before I went back into the room, shut the door, and returned the dowel to its place.

I didn't enjoy the view very much. It was too scary out there on that platform!

The next night we were in another hotel—one with railings around the balconies. This time when I went out to see the view, I leaned against the rail, lounged for a while in the cool breezes, and enjoyed myself tremendously.

What was the difference between the first night and the second? Safety! The second night I felt safe to enjoy the view because the balcony had rails to keep me from falling. This is how God's laws work for us. They are the rails around the balcony that give us the freedom to enjoy life. If you want to get the most out of life, begin by acknowledging the boundaries that have been established by the one who created life.

Think about it for a moment: What happens to the tires on your car if you keep running into curbs? It doesn't take long for them to get out of alignment. As a result, they become worn and last only a fraction of their intended life.

Some people believe they can treat their bodies the way such a careless driver would be treating the tires on his or her car. And then they have the nerve to complain to God when things go wrong with their bodies, just like the foolish driver who complains about the "cheap tires." But when we follow the laws of God, we are following the prescription for success and happiness. In other words, God's law isn't there to restrict us, but to free us to live life to the fullest.

Life by the Spirit

Admittedly, it takes a tremendous amount of strength and courage to live a godly life—especially in a world that often seems to reserve its highest accolades for people of dubious moral character.

The problems that exist within our society do not have to do with law so much as they have to do with a crisis of the spirit. As William J. Bennett writes:

> I submit to you that the real crisis of our time is spiritual. Specifically, our problem is what the ancients called acedia . . . an aversion to and a negation of spiritual things. . . . Acedia manifests itself in man's "joyless, ill-tempered, and self-seeking rejection of the nobility of the children of God." The slothful man hates the spiritual, and he wants to be free of its demands. The old theologians taught that acedia arises from a heart steeped in the worldly and carnal, and from a low esteem of divine things. It eventually leads to a hatred of the good altogether. And with hatred comes more rejection, more ill-temper, sadness, and sorrow. . . . Spiritual acedia is not a new condition . . . but today it is in ascendance.
>
> As individuals and as a society, we need to return religion to its proper place. Religion, after all, provides us with moral bearings. And if I am right and the chief problem we face is spiritual impoverishment, then the solution depends, finally, on spiritual renewal.
>
> The enervation of strong religious beliefs—in our private lives as well as our public conversations—has de-moralized society. We ignore religion and its lessons at our peril.[2]

I believe that Bennett has hit on the crux of the matter: The only way to live a morally upright life in today's society, the only way you can be an influence for good in society, is to "live by the Spirit."

Paul's brief letter to the Christians in Galatia is one of the New Testament's earliest books, probably written around 49 A.D. Paul wrote the letter because an argument was raging inside the church at Galatia regarding whether or not it was necessary for Christians to follow all of the Old Testament laws. Paul tells them that these laws have been replaced by a new, better, and more effective way of relating to God: being led by the Holy Spirit—the indwelling presence of God given to all believers. Paul says that though it may seem frightening at first to remove the constraints of the law, God's better way will produce a righteousness that the Old Testament law could never produce.

Paul explains that the law was only a temporary measure, a household slave charged with directing the immature until Christ should appear to reaffirm the ancient place of faith in the life of the believer. When Christ came, the law's usefulness ended. Instead, there is an exciting freedom—a freedom found in a new, direct relationship with God; freedom to live a truly good life.

In affirming freedom, Paul was not telling the Christians at Galatia that they should go on an orgy of self-expression. Instead, he was asking them to trust themselves to the Holy Spirit and to look to him to guide them. With new life in Christ and the indwelling power of the Holy Spirit, we can at last find the courage to be truly free—free from the old, sinful nature that used to control us and free to live in obedience to the guidance of the Holy Spirit as he calls us to act in love, to know and share joy, to experience and promote peace, and to otherwise develop within us the fruit of the Spirit.

In Israel during Paul's day people were searching for law and order. They wanted a moral code on which to base their lives and they believed they had found it in all of the laws of the Old Testament.

There were many difficulties associated with that sort of thinking, one being that people began to think that it was all right to do things that were unethical and even immoral, just so long as they were not strictly forbidden by the law. Some people tried to bend and stretch the law as far as it would go without breaking.

And so Paul wrote:

> The acts of the sinful nature are obvious: sexual immorality, impurity and debauchery; idolatry and witchcraft; hatred, discord, jealousy, fits of rage, selfish ambition, dissensions, factions and envy; drunkenness, orgies, and the like. I warn you, as I did before, that those who live like this will not inherit the kingdom of God.
>
> But the fruit of the Spirit is love, joy, peace, patience, kindness, goodness, faithfulness, gentleness and self-control. Against such things there is no law. Those who belong to Christ Jesus have crucified the sinful nature with its passions and desires. Since we live by the Spirit, let us keep in step with the Spirit.
>
> Galatians 5:19–25

The only way we can know for certain what to do is to be led by the Spirit of God, to be open to and willing to follow his direction. When you are led by the Spirit you will know the difference between right and wrong simply because you know. There may not be any written instructions to guide you in a particular area. There may not be any law regarding a certain situation. But you will know because the Spirit is leading you.

To see what I mean, go back for a moment and reread Paul's list of the "acts of the sinful nature." They are "sexual immorality, impurity and debauchery; idolatry and witchcraft; hatred, discord, jealousy, fits of rage, selfish ambition, dissensions, factions and envy; drunkenness, orgies, and the like."

Do you see anything illegal? I don't. There is nothing that will cause you to be hauled in front of a judge.

There's not even a misdemeanor here.

Nobody has ever heard, "Well, Mr. Jones, we'd like to hire you but we see that you've been convicted of hatred, jealousy and . . . oh, my . . . envy."

A few weeks ago I had what was, for the most part, a wonderful experience. I was able to attend a Barbra Streisand concert. I was thrilled because I've always loved the way that woman sings! But the evening became somewhat less pleasant for me when she sang the old song "Happy Days Are Here Again" as her tribute to the fact that abortion is legal in the United States.

She had every right to do that. Abortion is legal, and so by that standard, there's nothing wrong with it. And yet, it is an act that results in the loss of an innocent life.

It's this type of situation that causes me to say that our legal system cannot become a moral code for us today. Nobody can justify the legalization of abortion on the grounds that it's morally right. An argument in support of abortion can only be made on the grounds of a woman's rights. It is on this basis alone that our country allows a woman to abort the fetus that is infringing on her freedom.

Legality and morality are definitely not the same thing.

A Lesson from the Swallows

Think about nature for a moment. How do the salmon know how to swim upstream to spawn? How do monarch butterflies know how to fly back to Monarch Bay, where they were hatched? How do the swallows find their way back to San Juan Capistrano every spring?

Scientists can't explain any of these behaviors so they call them instincts. I believe "instinct" refers to a special knowledge God has placed within his creatures.

In the same way, I believe we have within us an innate instinct, which is, in reality, the guidance given by God's Holy Spirit. He is willing to communicate with us—to share the truth regarding every moral choice we need to make—if only we have demonstrated a willingness to listen and then to respond obediently to what he is telling us.

If you are listening, and if you are obedient, you will begin to demonstrate within your life these certain characteristics that Paul refers to as "the fruit of the Spirit." With these fruit in your life you can face any moral challenge.

Keep in mind that the society in which we live is not a moral society. It is a legal society, which is filled with selfish ambition and hatred and other forms of sinful lusts. But through the indwelling Holy Spirit, and the fruit that his presence can grow in your life, you can rise above all of these things to find the joy and strength that comes from living in peace with God. And there cannot possibly be a better, more fulfilling way to live.

Sadly, most people in our society, including many who profess to be followers of God, are not living that way, as the following story illustrates.

Does God Blink at Sin?

Leigh-Ann was thrilled when Roger asked her for a date. It wasn't his looks or his success in life that excited her, it was his character.

Roger was a deacon in the church Leigh-Ann had been attending for the past few months—a man of obvious spiritual depth. She had sat enthralled in a Bible study as he spoke with insight and clarity about difficult passages of Scripture. And when the man was called on to pray . . . well, a lot of people talk about a "personal relationship with God," but it was obvious that he really had one.

His prayers weren't like most prayers she had heard. They were like conversations with a best friend. He spoke to God as if he had intimate knowledge of the Creator. Not only that, but he prayed with eloquence, passion, and conviction too.

For so long Leigh-Ann had dreamed that a man like this might come into her life. She tried not to let her imagination run away with her, but it did anyway. As a longtime single mother with a ten-year-old son, she couldn't help but think about what a great husband and father Roger would make. She reminded herself that one date wasn't a lifelong commitment but still, in her mind's eye, she kept seeing the three of them doing things together. An image that consistently came to mind was of the three of them—she, Roger, and her son—sitting in church together, one happy family. That was something she had always dreamed of.

When date night finally came, the first thing Roger wanted to do when he came to her apartment to pick her up was pray about the evening ahead. He prayed that God would bless their time together, that they would have a good time getting to know each other, and that they might develop a friendship that would bring honor to him.

Then they headed out for the evening. And that's when he really began pouring on the charm. After dinner and some dancing, they went back to his house, where they spent the evening in bed together.

"I don't know how it happened, really," Leigh-Ann says, "but I tried to cover my guilt by telling myself that this was something that was beyond my control. Something that was meant to be."

Over the next few days and weeks, reality hit hard, like a sharp slap in the face. He didn't call. When he saw her at church he acted like he didn't know her. He wasn't cold, just indifferent. What had happened apparently was either no big deal or it was so humiliating that he could not consider pursuing the relationship.

She knew the Bible well enough to know that "Thou shalt not commit adultery" is one of the Ten Commandments. She remembered that Jesus had taught that any man who even looked at a woman in a lustful way was guilty of committing adultery with her in his heart. And hadn't Paul said that sexual sins were the worst sort of transgressions? What was going on here?

Over the next few weeks, she waited for some sign from Roger that he at least acknowledged what they had done together. But it didn't come. He apparently had no regret over the fact that he had sex with a woman he barely knew, nor did he seem to be at all concerned about the emotional distress that act was causing.

Leigh-Ann thought seriously about making a big deal about it. She wanted to confess to the entire church what they had done.

Ultimately, though, she decided to begin attending another church across town.

"I wish I had never gone to bed with him," she said.

If Diogenes were to walk the streets of 1990's America looking for an honorable man—or woman—would he be able to find one?

Have we deluded ourselves into thinking that God loves us so much that he will bless us no matter what we do—that it really doesn't matter what the Bible says?

I have enough faith in Christians to believe that, for most of us, the sins we commit are relatively small and inoffensive. But they are sins just the same, sins like:

   using the company telephone to make personal long-
      distance calls and never giving a second thought to
      whether it might be stealing
   telling a lie when the truth might get us into trouble
   reading questionable magazines and watching movies that
      are even worse

cheating on our income tax

drinking to excess

engaging in business practices that may not be illegal, but
most certainly are unethical

Remember, a sin is a sin. I'm not equating murder with the telling of a lie. But both are transgressions of morality, and if I want to live the life God wants me to live, if I want to live in a society that is just and secure, then I can tolerate neither in myself.

I believe that we have been tainted by the society in which we live. Jesus said, You are the salt and light of the world, to bring about positive change. But I'm afraid that far too many of us have given up on the idea of trying to make a constructive difference in the world and have, instead, let the world change us in ways that have taken us away from God.

A Few Words Not to Live By

"Do as I say, not as I do."

Have you ever heard anyone say that? More to the point, have you ever said it?

Many of us have done both. We've heard it from our parents. We've said it to our children. Those are famous words but certainly not good words to live by, especially not for anyone who wants to be pleasing to God.

How much better to be able to say, "Do as I say *and* do as I do." To live in such a way that, as Jesus said, people "may see your good deeds and praise your Father in heaven" (Matt. 5:16).

Wouldn't it be terrific to be able to look yourself in the mirror and know that you are living in a way that is pleasing to God? Wouldn't it be great to know that other people can come to know God because they can see him reflected in you?

In his book *Responsible Living in an Age of Excuses* Kurt Bruner asks why anyone should want to live a morally responsible lifestyle. He answers his own question this way:

> Lasting motivation for moral responsibility does come from the realization that it is the best lifestyle possible. Although it seems selfish, there is nothing wrong with doing right in order to obtain God's best for your life. He has revealed the path to fulfilled and successful living and wants us to take advantage of that knowledge.

He continues:

> I remain faithful to my wife because there are tremendous joys associated with a loving, committed relationship between a husband and wife. I could have more short-term excitement by pursuing numerous illicit affairs, but I would sacrifice long-term happiness in the process. That is a foolish and pointless trade!
> God is most glorified when we live fulfilled, successful lives . . . living consistently with God's plan for us as those created in His image. Viewing moral living as an opportunity to obtain God's best. . . . Although temptation still occurs, its appeal is diminished in light of the larger picture.[3]

I agree wholeheartedly. There is a great deal to be gained from living a morally responsible life.

I want to discuss what it takes to live such a life, determine why it's so important, and give you just a taste of the benefits that can be obtained from living the way God wants you to live.

If this book is successful, you will leave these pages with love at the center of your heart. You will trade the chains of the law for the bounty of the fruit of the Spirit: love, joy, peace, patience, kindness, goodness, faithfulness, gentleness, and self-control.

Are you ready?

PART 2

Nine Steps toward a Fulfilling Life

3

Step One
Love, the Foundation

I LOVE you, man!
Johnny

Admit it. The last place you expected to find a quote from a character in a beer commercial is in a book about the search for morality.

But the plain truth is that with that one line, Johnny became one of the best-known characters on television. Whatever you may think about beer, you've got to admit the guy's funny—uttering that one line with such sincere insincerity.

Johnny, as jerky as he may be, isn't all that far from reality. Sadly, there are a lot of people like him walking around in our world. I've met quite a few of them. I'd be willing to bet that you have too.

There are so many people who don't really have the slightest idea what love is all about but who are willing to sling the word around with reckless abandon in an attempt to get whatever they want. Think about how much better off this world would be if we all understood that love isn't really love at all if it's selfish and me-oriented.

I believe that most of us have been guilty at one time or another of misunderstanding and misrepresenting ourselves when it comes to love. Johnny says, "I love you" because he wants a beer. A teenage boy says, "I love you" because he wants his girlfriend to give in to his sexual desires. A little girl says, "I love you, Mommy" because she's done something wrong and doesn't want to be punished. The man in financial trouble says, "I love you" to God only because he hopes the Lord will help him find a way out of the mess he got himself into.

None of this has to do with love.

Some people confuse love with physical attraction. A man may think he loves a woman today because she looks so beautiful. But tomorrow, when she's having a bad-hair day or because she's not feeling too well and it shows, he doesn't feel quite the same way. That's not love. Not even close.

Some people think love is like a roller-coaster ride. You're on today, off tomorrow, back on the day after tomorrow. That's not love, either.

Others believe love is an emotion. They talk about "love at first sight" as if it's something that happens in an instant when your eyes lock onto someone else's eyes or when your heart is melted by the most magnificent smile you've ever seen. Those experiences are wonderful, yes, but they're not love.

Now that we've talked a little bit about what love isn't, let me tell you what it is:

Love is patient, love is kind. It does not envy, it does not boast, it is not proud. It is not rude, it is not self-seeking, it is not easily angered, it keeps no record of wrongs. Love does not delight in evil but rejoices with the truth. It always protects, always trusts, always hopes, always perseveres. Love never fails.

1 Corinthians 13:4–8

This type of love is the foundation of morality. It is the basis on which you can begin to construct the moral code for your life. It is the kind of love that the presence of God's Spirit can produce within you.

The Basis of Spiritual Maturity

When Paul wrote the words quoted above to the believers at Corinth, he was addressing a group of people who often interpreted the gospel through their traditional Hellenistic way of thinking.

One of the beliefs that was widely accepted throughout the Greek world of that day was that some people were especially close to the gods. Often this closeness involved bizarre behavior—trances, ecstatic speech, and other unusual manifestations. For example, a person with epilepsy was said to have the "divine disease," and the oracles at religious centers were often given drugs to bring on ecstatic utterances. The oracle at Delphi, for instance, breathed volcanic fumes that rendered her unconscious, and then her unconscious mutterings were interpreted by the priests.

It's not surprising then that the believers at Corinth were especially attracted to supernatural gifts—tongues, prophecy, and the like. As one might expect, they had come to view an exercise of supernatural gifts as a badge of worthiness.

Those who spoke in tongues considered themselves to be better than those who didn't. Those who frequently spoke in tongues thought themselves better than those who did so only occasionally.

In chapters 12 and 14 of the Book of 1 Corinthians, Paul spends a great deal of time speaking about such spiritual gifts. But sandwiched in between, in chapter 13, he makes clear that supernatural gifts are not the most important thing in the believer's life. They are not the mark of maturity nor of closeness to God.

It is love that is most important, and it is on the foundation of love that all else rests.

Paul even says the best supernatural gifts and abilities aren't really worth anything unless the person who has them also has love. If you want to measure true spirituality, Paul says, then look to kindness, patience, and those other practical expressions of real love.

What a Wonderful World This Would Be

Can you imagine what our world would be like if people had this kind of love in their hearts? We wouldn't need a police force. We wouldn't need a huge military budget. We wouldn't need to make sure our doors were locked when we were away from our houses. The people who make car alarms would be out of business. And it wouldn't be such a disturbing experience to read the morning newspaper or watch the evening news.

I remember an occasion about twenty years ago when my father and I were in Ismer, Turkey, waiting for a flight. We were sitting in the tiny terminal—a place that wasn't much bigger than the average living room—and all of a sudden we heard a tremendous roaring noise, and the entire building began to shake.

It wasn't an earthquake. All the noise and shaking were caused by three military-style jets roaring in for a landing.

As we watched them touch down, my father shook his head and said, "Isn't it terrible that we have to have these weapons of war? Everywhere you go in the world, you see them."

I nodded in agreement and said, "You know, Dad, God gives us the freedom to choose whether or not we're going to love. And as long as there are people who will decide not to love, we're going to need aircraft like these to protect those who want to love."

God's First Law

To love is the first and foremost law of God.

When Jesus was asked which was the greatest of God's commandments, he replied, "'Love the Lord your God with all your heart and with all your soul and with all your mind.' This is the first and greatest commandment. And the second is like it: 'Love your neighbor as yourself.' All the Law and the Prophets hang on these two commandments" (Matt. 22:37–40).

Those who choose to love God and others in this way are demonstrating spiritual morality.

Alan Loy McGinnis writes:

It is not original with me to observe that love is found not so much by those who are good-looking or witty or who have charismatic personalities, but rather by those who devote attention to love, who value it when they find it, and who nurture its growth in long-standing relationships. "Love never dies of a natural death," Anais Nin once wrote. "It dies because we don't know how to replenish its source; it dies of blindness and errors and betrayals. It dies of illness and wounds; it dies of weariness, of witherings, of tarnishings." And the author Robert Anderson says of love in marriage: "In every marriage more than a week old, there are grounds for divorce. The trick is to find, and continue to find, grounds for marriage."[1]

This, however, is not the choice everyone makes.

God gives us personal freedom in many areas of life, including the freedom to decide whether or not we're going to love the way he wants us to. So love begins with freedom, and with freedom comes responsibility.

At this point someone is bound to ask, "Well, why doesn't God just make us love other people?" God doesn't operate that way. He doesn't "make us" do anything . . . although he is certainly willing to give his help when we ask for it.

In Alcoholics Anonymous the first of the twelve steps is "I will admit that I am powerless over alcohol (my hang-up) and that my life is unmanageable." That is followed with "I will acknowledge that God is greater than I and that he can bring restoration to my life." It is through making this decision that you allow the power of God to run your life. You turn your will over to his will. As Jesus prayed in the Garden of Gethsemane, "Not my will, but yours be done" (Luke 22:42).

Love is a choice, just as it is a choice to surrender your will to God's will.

"Four Spiritual Laws," the little pamphlet published and distributed by Campus Crusade for Christ, gives an excellent picture of the difference between the life that is controlled by Christ and the life that is controlled by self.

God doesn't impose himself on us. He waits for our invitation. And once that invitation is extended, he, in his sovereignty, brings order and restoration. He helps us love as we ought to love.

Wouldn't it be terrific if everyone surrendered control of their lives to God? Wouldn't it be wonderful if we all consistently chose to do the loving thing? You may find it hard to like someone who mistreats you but you can make the choice to treat that person fairly and generously and thereby demonstrate your love for him or her.

I remember talking with a young woman who was riddled with guilt because she could not find it in her heart to love her father. It was easy to see why she felt that way. As far back as she could remember, her father had always told her that she was stupid, no good, and worthless. She couldn't remember anything she had ever done that had elicited a word of approval from the man.

As a married woman with children of her own, she lived several hundred miles away from her father. He was in his seventies and not in very good health, and she felt terrible because "daughters are supposed to love their fathers . . . and I don't feel anything for him."

But when I probed a little further, I discovered that she always called her father on his birthday and on Father's Day. She sent him cards and nice presents on those occasions and at Christmas. She saw him at least once a year, if at all possible. She was loving her father through her actions but berating herself because she didn't have the right feelings.

I believe that feelings can grow in a situation like that, with God's help and power. He can enable you to feel love for the most unlovely person.

But godly love is a choice. We demonstrate godly love for others through the way we act toward them. That young woman loved her father. Even if she didn't know it, she had made the choice to love him. Her actions were a demonstration of a personal morality built on a foundation of love.

I like what Judith C. Lechman has to say about the importance of such godly love:

> Full, gentle life in the Spirit is both a giving and a receiving of non-possessive, affirmative, and unselfish love involving God, others, and ourselves. Love is a force that binds us one to another and, most importantly, to God. Free of domination and control, love unites us while respecting our individuality and freedom.
>
> As the Spirit touches us and opens our hearts to divine love, we find ourselves reaching out with the glow of that same love to those around us.[2]

God Expects His Children to Love

I have four children—two girls and two boys—and one of the boys just turned thirteen. The day after his birthday I sat him down and said, "Bobby, you've just become a teenager. And because of that, I'm going to expect a lot more of you from now on." Then I outlined some of the additional responsibilities I expect him to carry out around the house.

Naturally I expect more from him than I do from his six-year-old brother. I might ask Bobby to mow the lawn or wash the car. But I'd never tell Anthony to go get the power mower out of the garage and cut the grass. Nor would I hand him a can of wax and tell him to go polish up the car. He would probably like it if I did, but because he's only six, the result might be disastrous.

In the same way, I'm more lenient with Anthony if he messes up his room or accidentally breaks something. No, I won't be happy with him and I'll find a way to discipline him but I won't expect him to act like he's thirteen, because he's only six! On the other hand, of course, I won't expect Bobby to act like he's only six, because he's thirteen.

God does the same thing with his people. The more mature we are, the more freedom he gives us and, simultaneously, the more responsibility he gives us. He expects us to make the choice to love and then through the fruit of the Spirit gives us the ability to love the way he wants us to.

It is often in loving others that we find renewed joy, enthusiasm, and, yes, love for ourselves. Alan Loy McGinnis tells this story:

> A wise minister I know was consulted by a widow who was feeling very sorry for herself at Thanksgiving time because she was alone and depressed. The pastor said, "I'm going to give you a prescription," and proceeded to write on a slip of paper the name and address of an old couple who were poor and ill with the flu. "These people are a lot worse off than you," he said bluntly. "Go do something for them."
>
> The woman went away muttering, but the next day she took a cab to the address she'd been given. There, in a tiny apartment, she found the couple. They were barely able to fix meals for each other and were frightened that one of them would have to enter a nursing home. So the woman arranged to take them Thanksgiving dinner. When she came back to see the minister the following week, she had new bounce to her step. "I hadn't fixed a turkey in years," she said. "But I shopped for all the trimmings and got up at 5:00 a.m. to put the bird in. When the taxi driver and I took it in to them, it was the best Thanksgiving I'd had in years."[3]

If only our society as a whole would learn the important lesson that there is joy and peace in loving and serving others! As Gloria Estefan sings: "Love, love, love, love, love/ misunderstood yet so desired/ we pay the cost for love, love, real love/ but we get back so much more, so much more."

Love Is the Higher Law

In the first part of this book I talked about the fact that God's laws are not always in agreement with man's laws—that they may be in direct opposition, in fact. This is certainly true when it comes to love. There are bound to be times when God's call to love compels us to break the laws of man.

During World War II a woman named Corrie ten Boom broke the laws of her native Holland to hide Jews from the authorities. Her country was under Nazi control, and Corrie knew that those Jews would probably be arrested, imprisoned, and even killed if she and her family turned them away. They chose the law of love over the law of man.

It was also during war that another Christian, a preacher by the name of Dietrich Bonhoeffer, came up with the concept of what we now call civil disobedience. Bonhoeffer was a native German who loved God and his country and he could not stand idly by, keeping his mouth shut while Hitler and his henchmen butchered innocent men, women, and children. The law of love compelled him to speak out, to do whatever he could to stop the slaughter.

He could have come to America, where he would have been free and safe to speak out against what was happening in his native land. In fact he was safely out of Germany at one point but he chose to go home and fight the Nazis face-to-face, not out of hatred for them, but out of love for those they were persecuting. As a result he paid with his life.

Bonhoeffer understood that we cannot be willing to obey laws that go against the principle of love. He could not turn away while the authorities arrested Jewish citizens and sent them off to death camps. Love would not let him do that.

Because Dietrich Bonhoeffer's personal morality was based on love, there were times when it compelled him to take a radical stand against his government. Bonhoeffer's actions resulted in his arrest and subsequent execution but he will be remembered forever as one of the great heroes of the Christian faith.

Are there parallels that could be drawn from this for Americans living in the last years of the twentieth century? I will leave that up to you. We could do so much if we based all of our decisions on a morality that springs first of all from love. Always remember that love is the higher law and the only true foundation for any lasting code of morality.

Let Love Flow through You

I know of a man who used to be filled with hate. He hated everyone who was different from him—especially blacks and Jews.

He hated them so much that he kept a gun tucked under the front seat of his car and he went around looking for an opportunity to use it, itching for a fight. It didn't matter what a person was like on the inside. If that person was black or Jewish, he hated him or her passionately.

His tendency toward violence eventually landed him in very serious trouble and he was sent to prison. It was there that he began reading the Bible. This fellow had always considered himself to be a Christian but somehow he had missed the fact that the message of the Bible is diametrically opposed to the kind of life he had been living.

The more he read the Bible, the more God's love began to penetrate his heart. He began to yield his pent-up hatred to God, asking the Lord to change him, however he saw fit.

Today this man, who once smoldered with hate, is the most loving, soft-spoken man you could ever hope to meet. The love of God seems to radiate from him. He pastors a racially mixed inner-city church and works tirelessly on issues related to racial harmony. The man's name is Tom Tarrants, and you can read his story in the book *He's My Brother*.[4]

He is a prime example of how God can change a man's heart, of how his love and power can flow through anyone who is yielded to him.

Frank Laubach, a great man of God, writes about a visit he made to an electric generating plant. The officials took him up to the top of a dam and showed him the huge turbines that have the capacity to produce an incredible amount of power.

But looking around at all the meters that measured how much electricity was being produced, Laubach saw that they all read zero. He didn't understand that and decided to ask his hosts about it.

"Here are all these incredible turbines," he said. "Here's this huge dam with the capability of producing tremendous amounts of electrical power . . . and yet there's no power being generated. What's going on here?"

The tour guide said, "It's because the valves are closed."

"Pardon me?"

"The only time we generate power is when the valves are open and the water flows through them. That spins the turbines, and the turbines begin to produce the electricity—the power. Until the valves are open, no electricity is being produced."

What I'd like you to see is that we are just like those turbines. Until we open the valves and allow God's Spirit to flow through us, love doesn't happen.

And so our first commitment and our first act of love needs to be to God. We love God and open ourselves up to his love, and then as it flows through us we can reach out and touch others with that love.

A proper moral code is not one in which a list is drawn up on a table of stone: "This is right, this is wrong, this is right, this other is wrong." That is legalism and it doesn't work. Jesus came to fulfill the Law (see Matthew 5:17). He taught that the fruit of the Spirit, produced in a Christian's life, perfectly fulfill the Law. Thus we must build our moral code on freedom, responsibilities, and commitments, and that's called love. When we do this, true morality unfolds.

Asking Some Tough Questions

If you feel that you have difficulty getting to the point where you can truly love others, if you feel blocked in some way, then it might help you to ask yourself some important and perhaps difficult questions and follow some suggestions. For example:

1. Can you think of some of the distorted ideas of love you've had to deal with in your life? If so, what were they, and how did your encounter with these counterfeit versions of love affect you?
2. Can you think of someone you have trouble loving? If so, what actions can you take to demonstrate godly love to that person? How do you think God would want you to act in this situation?
3. Remember these three truths about love:

   • Love is a freedom.
   • Love is a responsibility.
   • Love is a commitment.

   It may help you to think through your relationships, with other people and with God, and see where you are experiencing love in each of these three ways.

4. Reread the thirteenth chapter of 1 Corinthians and make a list of all the attributes of love Paul lists in that chapter. Then spend some time thinking about how God demonstrates all of those attributes in the way he cares for you. Consider, for example, the seventh verse. How is God's love demonstrated in the way he protects you, trusts in you, hopes in you, and perseveres with you?

5. Make a list of ways you could be more loving.

No, It's Not All Up to You

I want to make sure you understand that you cannot develop a loving attitude all by yourself. No, love is a supernatural gift from God, one of the fruit of the Spirit. That doesn't mean there isn't anything you can do to cultivate that fruit. It's important to be yielded to the Holy Spirit and to get yourself in the position where God is able to work through you.

What do I mean by that? You can block what God wants to do in your life by holding onto negative attitudes or by stubbornly refusing to change even though you know he wants you to. You may say, "Oh, come on, God, you can't expect me to love that guy. You don't know what he's done to me."

You know what? God does know what he or she has done to you, and he calls you to love him or her anyway.

It's not up to you to single-handedly change your life, to grit your teeth and say, "I'm gonna love that guy if it kills me!" It is up to you to get to the place where God can work through you and with you to help you become the loving person he wants you to be.

Once the fruit of love is growing strong in you, you'll be able to move on to the next step in the search for morality.

4

Step Two
Joy

The joy of the LORD is your strength.
Nehemiah 8:10

May the God of hope fill you with all joy and peace as you trust in him, so that you may overflow with hope by the power of the Holy Spirit.

Romans 15:13

Have you ever known anyone who was truly joyful?

I once knew a man who exuded joy in every situation. It really didn't matter what was going on in his life. The joy was always there. Certainly he wasn't always happy. He had some circumstances and problems, as we all do, that caused him hurt and pain. But through the worst of times, he was joyful. You could see that joy shining in his eyes. And you know what? That made him a joy to be around.

I've just made an important distinction between joy and happiness. They are related, yes, but they are not the same thing.

I started off chapter 3 by talking about what love is and what it isn't. Just as there are many misconceptions regarding the nature of love, so also are there misconceptions about the nature of this second fruit of the spirit—joy.

Happiness can be dependent on circumstances and it is fleeting. Happiness is what you feel when your boss tells you you've done a good job or when you get that raise you've been after for so long. Happiness is when your favorite team finally makes it into the World Series or the Super Bowl, when you're young and healthy and feel that you've got the world by the tail, when you drive off the lot in that beautiful brand-new car you've always wanted, when the most beautiful girl in the world says yes, she will marry you.

The kind of joy God wants you to have, the joy his Spirit can give you, is not dependent on circumstances like these. Joy can remain with you, even when happiness has flown away.

Joy can remain when your boss tells you that he's sorry, but there's just no money in the budget for raises right now. Joy can be with you when your favorite team is firmly entrenched in last place. Joy stays with you when you can feel that your youth is gone, when your bones ache or you're sick or you see now that you're never going to be the huge success in life you always thought you'd be, when that beautiful new car gets a big dent in it, when that gorgeous girl changes her mind and says she doesn't really want to spend her life with you after all.

In his book *The Power of Optimism* Alan Loy McGinnis cites Rose Kennedy as an example of someone who was able to hang on to joy despite the sorrows life brought to her:

> At age ninety-three, Rose Kennedy is being interviewed by a magazine reporter. By this time, four of her nine children have died violently. Another daughter, Rosemary, has been severely retarded all her life and will soon be gone. Mrs. Kennedy has outlived her husband long enough to have seen his rather profligate and

unscrupulous life told and retold in the press. She is an old lady, hit by tragedies again and again. The reporter asks about all this and Rose Kennedy says, slowly: "I have always believed that God never gives a cross to bear larger than we can carry. And I have always believed that, no matter what, God wants us to be happy. He doesn't want us to be sad. Birds sing after a storm. Why shouldn't we?"[1]

Joy, you see, is the internal understanding that God really is in control, that he loves you, and that he is working everything out in the best possible way, even during the moments when it doesn't seem much like it.

Joy is much stronger and deeper than happiness. It is the confident assurance that God loves you and is at work in your life, that he will be there for you no matter what may be happening right now.

Another important distinction is that happiness does not always contribute to personal morality. After all, it might be possible for me to be happy at your expense. Some people steal to get things that they think will make them happy. Other people smoke crack cocaine or inject heroin into their veins because it relieves the pain and gives them momentary happiness. Some even kill because they see murder as a way to get what they need to make them happy.

Joy, on the other hand, is an emotion that grows out of love: love for God, love for others, and love for yourself. Because joy has its roots in love, it is an emotion that wants to see itself replicated in other people. It is a sharing, helping, constructive thing. It is always beneficial and never harmful; always good, never evil. You might say that joy is happiness that has been born again.

One day Arturo Rivera was invited to play soccer at the Crystal Cathedral gym. He showed up to play but instead of bringing a soccer ball he brought his gun, which never left his side. He enjoyed the program and was impressed with the group of men who participated. One thing he noticed was that they were happy.

"Their faces radiated joy. It was then that I realized that I was different from them. I wanted what they had. Then it happened. It was an evening that I will never forget. My thoughts reflected on my daily life experiences and I began to think about God's love. The words that I heard from the other men seemed to touch me, and very simply I surrendered my life to God. I felt total freedom and my soul was renewed.

"I was aware of the gun hidden in my clothes and I told God that I would never use it again. I returned home a different person. I shared with my wife what had happened and she could not hold back her happiness. It was God's answer to her prayers. Our home was in ruins but God came and rebuilt it."

Today Arturo's life is very different. He is now a wonderful husband and father.

How to Have Joy

Shortly before his crucifixion Jesus told his disciples how to have joy in their lives:

> As the Father has loved me, so have I loved you. Now remain in my love. If you obey my commands, you will remain in my love, just as I have obeyed my Father's commands and remain in his love. I have told you this so that my joy may be in you and that your joy may be complete.
>
> John 15:9–11

Over the next six verses Jesus talks about the commands he expects his disciples to obey in order to remain in his love:

My command is this: Love each other as I have loved you. Greater love has no one than this, that he lay down his life for his friends. You are my friends if you do what I command. I no longer call you servants, because a servant does not know his master's business. Instead, I have called you friends, for everything that I learned from my Father I have made known to you. You did not choose me, but I chose you and appointed you to go and bear fruit—fruit that will last. Then the Father will give you whatever you ask in my name. This is my command: Love each other.

John 15:12–17

Joy comes as a result of trusting God and allowing him to love us and from living in obedience to his command to love one another.

God's love is unconditional and always waiting for you. If you are going to experience joy, you must choose to let God love you. When you open up your heart to him, he will fill you with his overwhelming love that can fulfill your deepest need and wash away your feelings of inadequacy and insecurity.

The Joy Within

There's an old song that says, "I've got the joy, joy, joy, joy down in my heart, down in my heart, down in my heart to stay."

There is great truth in the words of that old song. Joy is not something that comes from without—it's not something we chase after, like fun.

The United States Constitution guarantees to all American citizens a number of important rights, including a right to "the pursuit of happiness." Certainly, as you look around you, you're going to see a lot of people who are pursuing happiness with all their might. Joy isn't something to be pursued. Joy comes from within, from the hearts and souls of those who are secure in their understanding of God's great love for them.

The Importance of Self-Love

To have the kind of joy I'm talking about, it is necessary to love yourself. I am not talking about narcissism. When I say that you need to love yourself, I'm not talking about an "I come first" attitude. Self-love isn't the same thing as greed or self-promotion. It's not an attitude that manifests itself in looking out for number one or in disregard for anyone else's needs that may be in conflict with my own desires.

The self-love I'm talking about involves coming to see yourself as a creature of infinite worth because you were created in the image of God. It is coming to the point where you stand secure in God's love for you. After all, God loves you so much that he sent his Son to die for you. That means he sees you as someone of inestimable worth, and because that's how he sees you, that's also how you need to see yourself.

I believe one of the main problems in our society today is that people don't love themselves the way God wants them to. Consider the terrible problem of gang violence. Here in Southern California hardly a day goes by that we don't hear about some altercation between gangs. A drive-by shooting here. An innocent victim caught in the cross fire of a gang shootout there. Someone shot and killed for no reason at all except that someone thought he or she might be a member of a rival gang.

Why is all this happening? Certainly one of the reasons is because these kids don't love themselves. They see their lives as hopeless and without meaning. They reach the point where they don't care what happens to themselves or to anyone else.

Because they do not love themselves, they are not capable of loving others. Because they do not love themselves or others or God, they are living completely without joy. An absence of joy leads inexorably to death and destruction.

Many years ago, Dr. Robert Schuller—a man I usually refer to in more affectionate terms as "Dad"—wrote two books on self-love. The first book, which was titled *Self Love: The Dynamic Force of Success*, was written in the early 70s. When that book came out, Dad took a lot of heat. Some people were quick to blast the whole concept of self-love as being un-Christian.

Slowly, over the next few years, the importance of self-love became widely accepted, not only by theologians and religious people but by psychologists too. After all, it's hard to deny that Jesus gave us the command to love our neighbors as much as we love ourselves (Matt. 19:19). He wasn't giving a new command but merely quoting from the law of Moses (Lev. 19:18). If God doesn't expect us to love ourselves, it doesn't make any sense for him to use self-love as an example of how we're supposed to love others. So a few years later when Dad wrote *Self-Love: The New Reformation*, people were much more ready to hear and accept the message.

Seeing Ourselves through God's Eyes

The problem with loving ourselves is that most of us feel terrible every time we take a close look in the mirror. You may think you're too fat or too thin, or that your nose is too big or too small, or that your smile is crooked, and on and on and on. But really what I'm talking about is how we feel when we take a close look at the way we've lived our lives.

We see the sin. The immorality. The failures. The mistakes. Most of us are our own worst critics.

For example, Norman Vincent Peale threw out his first draft of *The Power of Positive Thinking* because he thought it wasn't good enough to be published. His wife, Ruth, rescued it before it was burned. It went on to become a classic best-seller that changed the lives of millions of people.

Leonardo da Vinci is quoted as having said, "I have offended God and mankind because my work didn't reach the quality it should have." Actress Elizabeth Taylor once told a reporter, "I hate to see myself on the screen. I hate the way I look. I hate the sound of my voice. I'm always thinking I should have played it better." When Dinah Shore was asked if she had any enemies, she replied, "I'm not crazy about me." Oh yes. And Abraham Lincoln told friends that he considered the address he gave at the Gettysburg battlefield "a flat failure."

These are only a few examples of people who were their worst critics, and I bring them up to tell you that you are not alone if you struggle with self-doubt and feelings of inadequacy. It may be true, as psychologist Alfred Adler said, "To be human is to feel oneself inferior." Many of us have grown up learning to be self-critical and berating ourselves for our failures—whether those failures are real or perceived.

That's not at all the way God sees you. He sees you as an individual created in his image. In God's eyes every human being has inestimable worth and value. It would be a great triumph of the human soul if we could come to view ourself as God does.

I'm not saying that God isn't hurt when we deliberately turn away from him, when we hurt others through our own acts of selfishness, or when we transgress his laws in some way. But he is always ready and willing to forgive, forget, and love us.

As the Bible says:

> I am convinced that neither death nor life, neither angels nor demons, neither the present nor the future, nor any powers, neither height nor depth, nor anything else in all creation, will be able to separate us from the love of God.
>
> Romans 8:38

Seeing yourself as God sees you and loving yourself the way he loves you will enable you to have joy in your heart.

Designed to Wear a Smile

One mistake that is made by a lot of Christians is thinking that God is a killjoy—that he doesn't want his children to have any fun. Nothing could be further from the truth. God wants us to be joyful and truly happy.

It's preposterous to think that God wants us to go around with long faces, passing judgment on anyone who seems to be having a good time. The truth of the matter is that the greatest joy a human being can possibly experience is to be in the presence of God, to be aware of the love and life of the Holy Spirit dwelling within.

What a tragedy it is to think that after God gave them life, a beautiful world to live in, and so many other wonderful blessings, a lot of people who profess to believe in him should walk around looking as if they just got the news they were being audited by the IRS!

God made us to be joyful. He designed the human face to wear a smile, and then by the gift of his Holy Spirit he gave us the joy to make us smile. It takes more than twice as many muscles to frown as it does to smile . . . so do yourself a favor, and smile!

Joy Smooths the Road to Success

In his best-selling book *Emotional Intelligence* Daniel Goleman tells of an experiment in which a group of athletes—swimmers in this instance—were tested to determine how they felt about themselves, whether they were optimistic or pessimistic by nature.[2]

Then, after they swam trial laps, their coach lied to them about the times they had recorded. He told them the performances they had turned in were not quite as good as they actually were and then urged them to try again.

Those who were more optimistic about themselves and their abilities almost always improved, whereas those who were pessimistic did worse the second time around. Why? Because the first group apparently had the "I-know-I-can-do-better" attitude, whereas the second group of swimmers thought the best performance they were capable of turning in had fallen short and so they tended to give up.

The book tells of a number of other similar experiments, all of them proving that joy, that assurance of God's love that brings confidence, can be a powerful contributor to personal success but that self-doubt and fear can contribute greatly to failure.

Alan Loy McGinnis writes:

Dr. George E. Vaillant has been following the physical and mental health of several hundred Harvard graduates since the mid 1940s. The data includes the results of extensive physical exams done every five years from age twenty-five through sixty. Ninety-nine of the men were rated by researchers as pessimistic, and they had markedly more illness between forty-five and sixty than the optimists. Curiously, a man's attitude at age twenty-five does not seem to affect his health for about twenty years. But if he has a robust body and good health at twenty-five, and also carries a bleak and cynical attitude, the researchers can predict that his health will begin to fall apart at middle age.

Other researchers studied a much more serious matter—sixty-nine women who had mastectomies for breast cancer. Three months after the surgery the women were asked how they viewed the nature and seriousness of the disease and how it had affected their lives. Five years later 75 percent of the women who had reacted with a positive, fighting spirit were alive, whereas less than half of those who reacted either stoically or helplessly were still alive.[3]

It would be hard to overestimate the importance of a joyful, cheerful outlook on life.

Get Off the Cycle of Blame

I wrote a book a few years ago that I wanted to call *Success Cycles*. But the word *success* is a non-90's word, so at the publisher's suggestion I dropped the title and called the book *Just Because You're on a Roll . . . Doesn't Mean You're Going Downhill*.

As I explained in that book, some people get rolling on a downhill run, and once that happens, it's hard to get it stopped. They get caught up in what we might call cycles of despair. They've become accustomed to feeling bad about themselves, to seeing themselves in a negative light, and they don't know how to stop such thinking.

They get caught up in inappropriate behavior and feel they are powerless to stop it. So they just ride along, going around and around and around again, doing the same old things they really don't want to do. They are caught in sexual immorality or trapped by alcohol and drugs. Pretty soon those people are looking for someone to blame for the sorry state of their lives. When you're looking for somebody to blame, you have three choices: God, others, or yourself.

You can blame God: "He's not taking care of me"; "This is the way he made me and I can't help myself"; "He's not giving me the strength I need to overcome this problem."

You can blame others: "They said some terrible things about me and that made me need a drink to feel better"; "I never would have gotten involved in this sin (whatever it is) if it hadn't been for them."

Or you can blame yourself: "I'm just no good."

None of these responses is productive. All of them are set-ups for more failure. If you think your problems are God's fault, you can't trust him to help you overcome them. If you blame other people for your problems, you can't go to them for the support they might give you. If you think your problems are all your own fault and that all you have to do is summon up enough strength and courage to do better, you're in trouble because you can't do it on your own.

Get on a cycle like that, and it is difficult to get off.

Get on the Cycle of Joy

Thankfully there's another cycle that is also hard to get off once you've begun riding, and that's the cycle of joy.

This cycle begins with faith in God. It involves believing, as Romans 8:28 teaches, that "all things work together for good" for those who love God.

Faith then moves on to forgiveness. That means believing that God loves you, that he cares for you, and that he forgives you. Do you remember when you were a teenager and you had an important date? What happened? Well, if your life was anything like mine, you probably woke up the morning of the big event with a huge, red, ugly zit right on the end of your nose.

When you looked at your reflection in the mirror, all you saw was that zit. It was like 90 percent of your body was a big pimple. Some little arms sticking out here . . . some legs here . . . a little face, and then a 130-pound zit.

I may be exaggerating a little but not much.

A lot of times when people look at the moral and spiritual fabric of their own lives, they see a lot of those big zits: all the failures, all the sins, all the wrong decisions—all the ways they have disappointed God, others, and themselves. But when you have faith that God forgives you, he erases the negative. He cleanses you and makes you pure, and once you have been for-given for what you've done, then you will find that you've gained the power to truly love—God, others, and yourself.

Ephesians 2:8–10 puts it this way:

> For it is by grace you have been saved, through faith—and this not from yourselves, it is the gift of God—not by works, so that no one can boast. For we are God's workmanship, created in Christ Jesus to do good works, which God prepared in advance for us to do.

This passage describes how you can get on the cycle of joy, learn how to love others as well as yourself, and then begin to demonstrate the framework of your life by doing good works. And so the cycle continues: Love produces more faith, which produces more forgiveness, which produces more love, and around and around it goes.

The Choice Is Yours

Think about these two cycles in financial terms. The cycle of blame is like running up huge debts on your credit cards. If you're not careful, interest adds up so fast that it just about buries you, and then it takes years to dig yourself out.

On the other hand, the cycle of joy is like a mutual fund. You put a little bit in as often as you can, leave it there to gather interest, and before you know it your money will be growing at an amazing rate.

In the first instance, the interest rate is working against you. In the second instance, it's working for you. The difference is where you stand in relation to the interest rate. Similarly, whether you are on the cycle of joy or the cycle of blame is largely dependent on where you stand in relation to God.

Remember Robert Frost's poem "The Road Not Taken":

> Two roads diverged in a yellow wood,
> And sorry I could not travel both
> And be one traveler, long I stood
> And looked down one as far as I could
> To where it bent in the undergrowth;
>
> Then took the other, as just as fair,
> And having perhaps the better claim,
> Because it was grassy and wanted wear;
> Though as for that, the passing there
> Had worn them really about the same,
>
> And both that morning equally lay
> In leaves no step had trodden black.
> Oh, I kept the first for another day!
> Yet knowing how way leads on to way,
> I doubted if I should ever come back.
>
> I shall be telling this with a sigh
> Somewhere ages and ages hence:
> Two roads diverged in a wood, and I—
> I took the one less traveled by,
> And that has made all the difference.

I love that poem and I think it's a great description of the choice that faces all of us at some point in our lives. We stand at the fork in the road, looking at two paths that go off in different directions, and we must make a decision as to which road we are going to follow.

We can choose to take the road of blame, which results in despair, a lack of faith, and failure; or we can choose to take the road of joy, which involves letting go and letting God, living by faith in his forgiveness and thereby experiencing the life-changing power of his love.

If you are on the cycle of blame, there's only one way to get off. That way is to come to God and say, "Okay, Lord, it's up to you. I can't do it by myself, so I'm asking you to help me."

Once you get on the right road—the right cycle—you'll be able to sing that old song and really mean it. You'll have the joy, joy, joy, joy down in your heart, down in your heart, down in your heart to stay.

Taking Some Steps toward Joy

Here are a few ways you can begin to build a healthy self-love and respect and so begin to open yourself up to the joy God wants to build in you:

1. Take a few moments to make a list of your good qualities. (You may want to ask your significant other or another person you feel safe with to answer some of these for you.) What do you do particularly well? What traits and strengths do other people seem to admire in you? What unique qualities do you have that make you a special person?

2. Draw up another list—things you don't like about your-self. Are there particular steps you can take to improve yourself in these areas?

3. People who spent their childhood in a negative and crit-ical atmosphere have a hard time learning to love them-selves. Is this true of you? If so, what steps can you take to prove wrong the negative and critical things that have been said to or about you?

4. An unforgiving attitude can prevent you from being joyful. Is there someone you are unable to forgive? If so, what keeps you from forgiving that person? What would it take for you to be able to forgive that person? What do you think God wants you to do in this situation? Have you asked him to help you forgive? If not, why not do it now? A failure to forgive will hurt you more than it will hurt the subject of your anger.

5. In John 15:9 Jesus says, "As the Father has loved me, so have I loved you. Now remain in my love." What does it mean to live in God's love? What do you need to do to get to the point where you are living in his love?

Joy is not something you can achieve by your own effort. It is one of the fruit that will be produced within you by the indwelling Holy Spirit. But it is not God's way to take you by the shoulders and shake you and make you joyful even if you don't want to be! He wants to work with you, and if you'll get yourself in a position where he can do that, you'll be amazed at the changes he brings into your life!

5

Step Three
Peace

Peace is not an absence of war, it is a virtue, a state of mind,
a disposition for benevolence, confidence, justice.
Benedict de Spinoza

It doesn't take a scholar to tell you that peace is hard to
come by.

Take a trip around the world and you'll find many places
where peace is a desperately desired—but absent—quality. In
the Middle East citizens pray daily for peace, but it does not
come. Over the past few years war has killed thousands of
people in Bosnia, and as I write these words, fighting rages in
Sudan and Liberia. By the time this book goes to the publisher a few weeks from now, it is possible that several other
wars will have erupted in various countries around the globe.

All of these wars give tragic evidence to the lack of peace
that pervades the hearts of men.

Think about how many wars our country has been involved in:

- War for Independence
- War of 1812

- Mexican War
- Civil War
- Spanish-American War
- World War I
- World War II
- Korean War
- Vietnam War
- Desert Storm

Then there have been dozens of little skirmishes here and there as our troops have gone into the Dominican Republic, Panama, Grenada, and assorted other countries as "peace-keepers."

I'm not making a judgment as to whether our involvement in any or all of these wars was right or wrong. I'm just showing that peace is awfully hard to come by.

Perhaps you have seen the movie *Braveheart*, which won the Academy Award for Best Picture in 1995. It is an excellent movie about William Wallace, who led Scotland's revolt against England in the early 1300s. It's also a disturbing film because it is extremely violent. Apparently it's an accurate depiction of the way things were back in those days, with opposing armies slaughtering each other on the battlefield. You would have to have a pretty strong stomach not to be affected by watching all the blood that flows in that movie.

As I watched *Braveheart*, I couldn't help but think that we human beings have not really come very far in the last six-hundred-plus years. We're still slaughtering each other. The only thing that's changed is the technology.

What makes it even worse is the fact that we are learning how to kill our enemies in ever-increasing numbers. For example, if you look at statistics from the Revolutionary War, you'll find that only about three thousand American soldiers were killed in nearly six years of fighting. Today one nuclear exchange could result in millions of deaths.

In fact throughout the world today war is one of the top killers of children. In its *State of the World's Children* booklet for 1995, UNICEF writes:

> At one time, wars were fought between armies; but in the wars of the last decade far more children than soldiers have been killed and disabled. Over that period, approximately two million children have died in wars, between four and five million have been physically disabled, more than five million have been forced into refugee camps, and more than twelve million have been left homeless.
>
> These are statistics of shame. And they cast a long shadow over future generations and their struggle for stability and social cohesion.[1]

I don't mean to depress you but I do want you to have an accurate understanding regarding the world we live in. These sad statistics are a reflection of a world that has not known peace since Cain killed Abel.

Some Wars Are Personal

Not all wars are waged on a battlefield with bombs and bullets. Some are wars of words waged between husbands and wives who have forgotten how to love each other. When a man and woman live together as husband and wife, they get to know each other very well. Each spouse knows how to do the little things that bring pleasure to his or her partner—and they also know what will really hurt each other. A tragedy of human nature is that some people will use information they have about you that can really hurt you.

If the husband knows his wife is sensitive about her weight, then what do you suppose he is going to say in the heat of an argument? He may say something about being glad he doesn't have to carry her over the threshold these days.

If the husband is sensitive about losing his hair or about getting passed over for the big promotion at work, it's going to take a very good woman not to go after him in these vulnerable areas, especially if he's been attacking her sore spots.

Yes, every marriage has its little spats. That's just part of living together through the frustrations of daily life. But if men and women who swore to love each other until death do them part often find that their relationship has deteriorated to the point that their marriage resembles the movie *The War of the Roses*, then what hope is there that the rest of us can get along? What hope is there when similar wars are fought between parents and their children or between brothers and sisters?

There is hope only in God.

Peace is available through faith in God and through the power and presence of the indwelling Holy Spirit. The fact is that you will never have external peace without internal peace.

What I mean is that as long as men and women do not have peace inside of them—the peace that only God can give—there are going to be wars of various types: wars between husbands and wives, between parents and children, between people of different races and cultures, and between countries. Only when I have God's Spirit within me, can I live in true fellowship with my neighbor.

I like very much what C. S. Lewis has to say in *Mere Christianity*:

> Almost all people at all times have agreed (in theory) that human beings ought to be honest and kind and helpful to one another. But

though it is natural to begin with all that, if our thinking about morality stops there, we might just as well not have thought at all. Unless we go on to the second thing—the tidying up inside each human being—we are only deceiving ourselves.

I do not mean for a moment that we ought not to think, and think hard, about improvements in our social and economic system. What I do mean is that all that thinking will be mere moonshine unless we realize that nothing but the courage and unselfishness of individuals is ever going to make any system work properly. It is easy enough to remove the particular kinds of graft or bullying that go on under the present system: but as long as men are twisters or bullies they will find some new way of carrying on the old game under the new system. You cannot make men good by law: and without good men you cannot have a good society. That is why we must go on to think of the second thing: of morality inside the individual.[2]

All You Have to Do Is Surrender

How can you achieve the "morality inside the individual" that Lewis writes about? By surrendering your life to God. When you do that, you will obtain and experience an internal peace, a peace of the soul.

When God called the children of Israel out of Egypt, he gave them the Pentateuch, the books of Law that make up the first five books of the Bible: Genesis, Exodus, Leviticus, Numbers, and Deuteronomy. After that for thousands of years anyone who wanted to have peace with God had to follow the laws contained in those books. The problem was that human nature fails. There was never a single human being— with the lone exception of Christ—who ever got through life without breaking at least one of God's laws. Whenever a law was broken, the peace was broken. Trying to obtain peace through the law always resulted in failure.

But then God sent his Son, Jesus Christ, into the world to provide a new and better way for people to live in peace with God and with each other. Jesus was not sent into the world to abolish the law but to fulfill it, to resolve the dilemma that God has always had in his relationship with us fallible, sinful humans. You see, God is full of grace and mercy but he is also a God of law and justice. Because of that, there is always tremendous tension between law and grace.

Some people get upset about the fact that God requires justice—payment for sin. But think for a moment how you would feel if God just winked at everything that happened and said, "That's okay. I forgive you." Wouldn't you be upset if you thought that God had looked down on Adolf Hitler massacring millions of innocent Jews and said, "Well, I don't like it too much but I guess boys will be boys"? I know I would. It makes me feel good to know that ultimately, in every situation, justice will prevail.

Just look around you at all the crime and violence, at people getting away with all sorts of things and then walking away without so much as a slap on the wrist. Isn't it good to know that God is a God of justice? Nobody is really going to get away with anything, because God will demand payment.

But the problem is that we're all guilty, and so sooner or later we're all going to have to pay for our crimes. Your sins may not be as violent as other people's sins. You may not be a murderer or a thief. But in God's eyes sin is sin and sin requires punishment, regardless of the degree of sin.

So what did God do? He provided a way through which we can have our crimes paid for, and that is by accepting the sacrifice of Jesus Christ, who died on the cross on your behalf and mine. When Jesus was nailed to the tree, he was a completely innocent and sinless man, but he took upon his own body the punishment that should have been meted out to you and me.

That is what we mean when we say that Jesus came to fulfill the law—to bring it to completion. We cannot have peace by living in obedience to the laws of Moses, but we can have peace through faith in Christ and his sacrifice on the cross. What's more, when you surrender your life to God through faith in Christ, you receive the gift of the indwelling Holy Spirit, and it is the Holy Spirit who cultivates the fruit of the Spirit within you.

Now, of course, having faith in Christ doesn't free you to do anything you darn well please. You can't put on a mask and go rob the corner convenience store and then think, *It's okay because I have peace through Christ.* No, you try as hard as you can to live in obedience to God's laws but you realize that when you fail, Jesus will be there to help you overcome. You realize that you do not have to remain in failure.

It's like trying to swim from California to Hawaii. If you are a good swimmer you might be able to swim thirty or even one hundred miles. But then you start to get tired and the waves get rougher. You don't think you have it in you to make one more stroke. You're so tired and discouraged that you can't even dog-paddle and so you start to sink. But no sooner does that happen than Jesus is right alongside you in his lifeboat. He pulls you in and says, "I'll take you the rest of the way to Hawaii." Which he does. Sitting in that lifeboat, you are totally at peace!

The Paths of Peace

What has happened is that you have secured peace with God and are obtaining peace with your fellow human beings because you have taken the first steps of a journey along what I call "The Paths of Peace." By following these steps, you will be able to find peace first of all with God, then with yourself, and finally with other people. These are twelve steps that help people grow personally and spiritually. They are adapted from the Twelve Steps of Alcoholics Anonymous and form the outline of my book *Dump Your Hang-Ups*.

1. Admit that you are powerless over your sinful nature and that your life has become unmanageable. You've gone as far as you can on your own and it just wasn't far enough.

2. Believe that there is a power greater than yourself that can restore you. This is when you acknowledge God's existence, when you say, "God, I know you're there, and I know that I need your help."

3. Make a decision to turn your will and life over to God's care. Here you decide to take the step of asking for God's help, to "let go and let God," realizing that he can bring you through situations in life that would otherwise destroy you.

When that is done, you will have peace with God, which means you will also have peace within your soul.

Once you have made peace with God, the time has come to make peace with yourself.

4. Take a fearless moral inventory of your life. Why did I use the word *fearless?* Because it may not be easy to take a long, hard look at your life, especially when you're paying close attention to all the ways you've fallen short of who and what you want to be.

Taking a moral inventory requires more than fifteen or twenty minutes. It requires getting out pen and paper and writing down everything you can think of about your moral past that hasn't been what it should be. List everyone you have hurt, offended, or violated in some way. This is emotionally difficult but very worthwhile.

Think of it as preparing to do a major spring-cleaning of your house. Before you get started, it's important to take stock of the situation and decide what areas need special attention—screens cleaned, windows washed, and so on. You can't clean up the tarnished areas in your soul until you find out where they are.

5. *Admit your sins to yourself, to God, and to another human being.* This is really difficult.

First of all, look over your list and acknowledge, "Yes, I am guilty of all of these things."

After that, sit down with God and go over your list with him. You don't have to talk to him in Latin or use fancy words. Just open up your heart and tell him what he already knows: that you have all of these problem areas in your life and that with his help you are going to deal with them. It may help you to realize that God is always ready to listen and forgive.

The third part of this step is the toughest of all. It's not easy to sit down with a living, breathing human being and tell him or her about all your faults and weaknesses. But this step is very important because you need the support of another person. God designed us so that we need each other, and that is why he has given us the commandment to "carry each other's burdens" (Gal. 6:2). It is liberating to be able to share your weaknesses with another person and have them love you anyway. This is part of the cleansing process in which you are set free of the hold these wrongs have over you. Thus it is an important step along the path to personal peace.

6. *Prepare your heart for God to remove all of these flaws and sins from your life.* How do you do this? Spend some time thinking about all of the ways these problem areas have affected you and those you love. Pray that God will help you get to the point where you really want to be set free.

Do you recall what St. Augustine prayed when he was a young convert to Christianity? "Lord," he prayed, "give me chastity . . . but not yet." He knew he needed to change the way he was living but he wasn't ready to do it.

Sorry, that won't work. If you have a problem in any area, whether it's sexual temptation, alcohol, drugs, gambling, or anything else, you need to get to the point where you're willing to give it up. With God's help, you can.

So pray, meditate, contemplate . . . do whatever it takes to get you there.

7. *Humbly ask God to remove from your life all your failures, sins, and shortcomings.* Simply go to him in prayer, talking to him in your own words, asking him to remove these problem areas. You don't have to ask twice. Ask in faith, and he will do it.

Once you've done that, you have established peace with yourself and with God. Now it's time to begin establishing peace with other people.

But before you do that, please make sure that you have gone through the previous seven steps. If you haven't, you're not going to be ready spiritually or emotionally to handle steps eight and nine.

Remember that before you can get your relationships with other people squared away, you must first get your relationship with God right and that takes time. Then you have to get your relationship with yourself right, and that too takes time. Only when you are right with God and yourself, are you ready to start changing your relationships with other people.

8. *Make a list of all the people you have harmed and prepare yourself to make amends with them.* Can you think of some people you don't talk to? Or some who won't talk to you? Is there someone you would cross the street to avoid? Well, it's time to change all that. It's time to put up the white flag and declare a truce. It's time to put an end to war—on both the global and personal levels.

Please note that this step does not involve going out and making amends with people, but rather *being willing* to make amends. You are simply making a list of all the people who should hear you say, "I'm sorry" or who need to see you start living the way you've always known you ought to live. You might even need to take specific steps to undo some damage you've done. None of this will be easy to do and that's why you need to prepare your heart, asking God to help you humble yourself enough to confront those you have hurt by your actions.

By now you may be thinking that these Paths of Peace aren't so easy to follow. I have two things to say about that:

- Peace is worth the price.
- With God's help, it can be a lot easier than it sounds.

9. Follow through on the preparation you made in step eight. That's right. The time has come to track those people down and do your best to make things right with them. If some people are so angry with you that they won't even talk to you, that's their problem, not yours. The important thing is that you make a serious, sincere effort to make things right. You are not responsible for how others react to your overtures.

What if you have wronged someone who is no longer living? Sit down and write that person a letter, explaining what you did wrong and asking for forgiveness. Then ask God to help you obtain freedom, release, and forgiveness in that instance.

If you have sincerely followed these first nine steps, you will be at peace with yourself, with God, and with others. The final three Paths to Peace are what I refer to as "maintenance measures."

10. From now on, whenever you do something wrong, promptly admit it. This is really an extension of the fourth step. It is taking a fearless moral inventory of your life on a continual basis. Don't let those sins build up again. As soon as you see yourself doing something wrong, admit it and get rid of it before it causes serious damage.

As the Bible says, "If we confess our sins, he is faithful and just and will forgive us our sins and purify us from all unrighteousness" (1 John 1:9).

11. Seek to improve your conscious contact with God so you can discover his will for you. Pray. Meditate. Read the Bible. Do everything you can to get closer to God so you can understand how he wants and expects you to live. Ask him for power and strength to do what he wants you to do. He'll give it to you.

12. Tell other people about what has happened to you. It's important for you to tell others how you found peace so they can obtain it for themselves. Imagine what this world would be like if we all were at peace with God, ourselves, and one another. As the old Sam Cooke song says, "What a wonderful world this would be!"

Morality begins with love, continues with joy, and then deepens as we learn to live in peace with God, ourselves, and others. It is a wonderful thing to live in peace, to be able to put your head down on your pillow at night and go right to sleep, resting securely in God's love.

Additional information on how these twelve steps can help you overcome your problems can be found in my book *Dump Your Hang-Ups . . . without Dumping Them on Others* (Revell). This book is also available in a workbook format.

6

Step Four
Patience

Have patience, have patience,
Don't be in such a hurry.
When you get impatient,
You only start to worry.
Remember, remember,
That God is patient, too.
And think of all the times that others
Have to wait for you!
                    The Music Machine

It was just before midnight when the call came in to the Los Angeles County Sheriff's Department. A young man said that he and his girlfriend were worried about another couple with whom they had been double-dating. He explained that the four friends had been returning from dinner, driving along the Pacific Coast Highway, when they had decided to take a detour up one of the side roads in the Point Dume area—a place where rocky cliffs rise straight up from the ocean at several points.

The missing couple was feeling adventurous and wanted to explore one of the rocky outcroppings overlooking the ocean. When the other couple didn't want to join them, they had laughingly called out that they would be back within fifteen or twenty minutes. Then they headed up the trail, quickly disappearing into the darkness.

Forty-five minutes later, when there was no sign of the adventurous duo, the other couple had begun to get annoyed. Another fifteen minutes went by and that annoyance had turned into full-blown anger. But now that anger had given way to fear. Something had to be wrong.

There was a full moon that night, but its light was more than occasionally obscured by a layer of clouds rolling across the Southern California sky. This was not a good night to go exploring, especially in an area where one false step could send you plummeting toward the water more than one hundred feet below.

The report that someone might be in trouble off the Malibu coastline was quickly relayed to the Aero Bureau, and a patrol helicopter was sent to check out the situation. On board the McDonald-Douglas 500 E patrol helicopter were George Green and Dave Skinner, two officers with twenty years of flying experience between them. They would work in tandem with rescue crews on the ground. It was the helicopter crew's job to locate the missing couple and then guide ground personnel in carrying out the rescue.

It took several minutes before the helicopter's big searchlight came across anything out of the ordinary. But finally George saw something and called for his partner to swing the chopper in for a closer look.

There they were, perched precariously on a small ledge about twenty feet down the side of an almost perpendicular cliff. Apparently, walking in the darkness the couple had come too close to the edge of the cliff. It looked like the ground beneath their feet had given way, sending them tumbling down. They were alive only because this small outcropping had stopped their fall—otherwise they would have plunged into the water below.

As it was, there was no way for them to climb back up to the top of the cliff. And there was no guarantee that the small ledge on which they sat was going to hold up for very long.

It was going to take at least forty-five minutes to make the rescue. In the meantime the helicopter had to stay as close to the frightened couple as possible. The ground team needed the helicopter's searchlight to stay focused on the couple's location, and when the team arrived at the top of the cliff, they would need George's instructions to guide them to the exact spot where the couple was waiting.

It was all Dave could do to hold the copter steady in the winds blowing in from the ocean but somehow he managed, even though his arms ached from the struggle. He had to keep his eyes fixed on a point on the horizon in order to keep the craft hovering in the same location. Meanwhile the weather seemed to be getting worse. Those clouds in the sky were getting thicker and darker, and the wind was definitely picking up. The weather or something else seemed to be hampering the ground crew's efforts too. Forty-five minutes had come and gone, and they were still not in position to make the rescue.

As for George, he kept the observer's light trained on the young couple. He didn't move a muscle, even though his arms were cramping and sweat was running down the back of his neck. Oh, how he wanted to take a few moments to stretch, to wipe the sweat away—but if he did, it might take him a while to regain his bearings, to relocate the victims, and every second was important. George realized just how true that was, as out of the corner of his eye he caught a glimpse of the fuel gauge and realized that if the rescue didn't happen very quickly, they were going to have to send out another team to fish Dave and him out of the water.

Finally the rescuers arrived at the top of the cliff. One detective would rappel down to the victims and get them fitted in harnesses. Then they would be hoisted to the top, wrapped in thermal blankets, and treated for exposure and any injuries they might have suffered.

Patiently, George guided the detective to the right spot. "About three feet to your left now. . . . That's it . . . just a little bit further. Okay . . . you're almost there. A little more to your right," and so on. By the time the rescue was complete, the "fuel low" light was burning brightly.

The helicopter made it back home with less than ten minutes of fuel to spare.

When I heard this true story, I thought about how important it is for the men and women who work on rescue squads to have patience. Without it, the job would not be done effectively, and many lives would be lost.

But really, patience is important everywhere, in all walks of life. From time to time we all get "stranded" on some treacherous shores of life. Patience provides a way of escape.

In fact if I were asked to name the most important qualities a human being can have, patience would be very near the top of the list. Patience makes possible all sorts of accomplishments. The biblical view of the importance of patience can be seen in this verse from the 16th chapter of Proverbs: "Better a patient man than a warrior, a man who controls his temper than one who takes a city" (Prov. 16:32).

Living in an Impatient World

Patience, the fourth fruit of the Spirit, is an important ingredient for building a personal code of morality. It is one of the keys to a better life.

Sadly, in the frantic world of the 1990s patience is in very short supply. Sometimes it seems that the faster we're able to go, the more impatient we become.

Have you ever seen someone standing at a fax machine urging the pages to go through faster, or hear them say, "We've got to get a new fax because this one is too slow"?

Do you know people who upgrade their computer system every time something newer and faster comes out or who complain about the system they have because it's "just too slow"?

This age of microwaves, fast food, and coast-to-coast airline flights is not conducive to the development of patience. But if you really listen, sometimes, in the midst of all the hurry, you can hear God's voice whispering, "Slow down! Take it easy."

I'm sure you've heard it said, "No pain, no gain." That statement is used a lot of different ways but most often concerning the benefits that come from physical exercise. It hurts to keep your body fit. If you've let yourself go and then decide that you want to get into shape, it can really hurt.

There's no way to tone those muscles, flatten that stomach, and reduce that percentage of body fat other than to keep going until it hurts. There's no magic elixir that will suddenly make you able to run a four-minute mile or bench press two hundred pounds.

It takes hard work and patience to get yourself in shape physically, mentally, and spiritually.

Patience: A Key to Maturity

What exactly is patience? In the Bible it's almost always tied together with endurance, as in the patient suffering of Christ as he went to his death, and of Job before him.

Webster defines it as "the capacity, habit or fact of (1) bearing pain or trials calmly or without complaint; (2) manifesting forbearance under provocation or strain; (3) not hasty or impetuous; and (4) steadfast despite opposition, difficulty or adversity."

I wouldn't go so far as to say that patience is the key to becoming a perfect human being, but without patience you can never be who and what God wants you to be; you can never accomplish all the things God wants you to accomplish; and you certainly cannot construct a moral foundation on which to build the rest of your life.

How much patience do you have at home, on the job, when you're driving in rush-hour traffic? Are you patient when your spouse is in a talkative mood, even though you'd really like nothing better than to spend an hour or so alone with the newspaper? Are you patient with the children when they have to play indoors because it's raining and they keep demanding your attention and keeping you from the important things you have to do?

Have you ever demonstrated by your behavior that you are not a very patient person? Have you ever "gone off" on someone and then later regretted your actions, wishing you could have kept yourself under control? Most of us, if we're totally honest with ourselves, will agree that we have all been embarrassed or hurt at one time or another by a lack of patience, either as victims or perpetrators.

Patience may be one of the rarest commodities in the world today. As with most rare things, it is of incredible value.

How to Obtain Patience

Patience is required of those who would obtain the best of God's blessings. That immediately brings to mind a vitally important question, namely: How do you get patience?

I believe there are at least four specific ways you can obtain patience.

1. Ask for it.
2. Don't get hung up on details.
3. Don't give in to discouragement.
4. Have a proper perspective of time.

1. Ask for it. The first of these four ways is the most obvious. Take a close look at your life and you are bound to see a particular problem area (or areas) in which you are sorely lacking in patience. Perhaps you have patience with everyone else's children but not with your own. Perhaps you're impatient with your spouse, your boss, or when you're stuck in rush-hour traffic.

You might start off by asking God to give you more patience in general but then pray more specifically about those difficult areas where you really need his help. Then continue to pray about specific situations as they arise. Learn to view challenging situations as opportunities to grow, to acquire the patience God wants and expects you to have. Don't worry too much if you blow it once in a while. This is a growth process, and one person who will really need your patience as you're going through it is you!

2. Don't get hung up on details. In other words, try not to let minor matters bog you down. Concentrate instead on the overall view of what God is doing in your life.

I'm sure you've heard the saying, "That was the straw that broke the camel's back." That means that things piled up and piled up to the point that one more little insignificant item precipitated a disaster. Similarly, when a person is trying to learn patience, it's usually the little things that will trip up him or her.

Consider the patience of Christ as he stood before Pilate. He didn't lash out angrily at those who were accusing him. He didn't demand that he be given a chance to cross examine those who had testified against him. He didn't react impatiently or impetuously to what was happening to him, because he knew that the big picture included his atoning death on the cross.

But don't ever get the idea that Jesus was demonstrating a passive, "do-whatever-you-want-with-me" attitude. Not at all. His was an active, aggressive patience that was necessary to accomplish his earthly mission. Sometimes it is far harder to be patient in the face of adversity than to lash out and defend yourself.

Of course the biggest part of the big picture is knowing that God has a plan for your life and that his plan is for your good, no matter what your circumstances may be right now.

Jesus said that the meek would inherit the earth. Well, the meek are those who hang on because they understand that God is the true author of all opportunity. They are patient because even if they are forced to let go, they know that God won't let go of them. They see the big picture.

3. *Don't give in to discouragement.* It's not easy to wait for God's blessing, but waiting is a spiritual principle. How do you wait? Primarily by keeping your eyes on God and knowing that he will bring you through any trial. If you are a child of God, then his promise through the prophet Isaiah belongs to you:

> Fear not, for I have redeemed you;
>   I have summoned you by name; you are mine.
> When you pass through the waters,
>   I will be with you;
> and when you pass through the rivers,
>   they will not sweep over you.
> When you walk through the fire,
>   you will not be burned;
>   the flames will not set you ablaze.
>   Isaiah 43:1–2

The Bible contains many examples of men and women who patiently accepted the trials that came their way. They could do so because they knew that the Lord was with them, and that knowledge kept them from becoming discouraged.

Remember Joseph, who was sold into slavery by his own brothers and cast into prison on false charges? He knew that even there in the prison God was with him and that his present circumstances would not keep him from accomplishing great things.

The story of how Joseph was lifted out of adversity to become the second-most-powerful man in all Egypt is one of the most inspiring accounts in the entire Bible. Remember how his brothers came to Egypt during a time of drought to buy food and how, after testing them to see if they had changed, Joseph revealed himself to them? They stood before him trembling, and with good reason. They remembered what they had done to him; they were afraid he wanted to get even with them—and if anybody was ever in a position to exact revenge it was powerful Joseph.

But what did he say to his brothers? "Don't be afraid. Am I in the place of God? You intended to harm me, but God intended it for good to accomplish what is now being done, the saving of many lives. So then, don't be afraid. I will provide for you and your children" (Gen. 50:19–21). Here was a man who was able to resist discouragement and avoid defeating himself through impatient and impulsive actions by keeping his eyes on God.

Maybe you are in a prison of some kind, perhaps a prison of the mind, body, or emotions. Perhaps someone who means the world to you has just told you that he or she doesn't love you anymore. Your spouse has asked you for a divorce and your life has come crashing in on you.

Could it be that the doctor has given you the devastating news that you have a serious illness? Perhaps he has told you that you have cancer or AIDS or something else just as frightening and just as life-threatening. Maybe you've lost your job and don't know where you're going to find another one.

When you're going through situations like these, how in the world can you resist discouragement? You can do it by keeping your eyes on God, remembering that he loves you and that he can and will make all things work together for your ultimate good (Rom. 8:28).

I'm not saying you should paint a plastic smile on your face and go around in a state of denial, refusing to admit that anything bad has happened to you. When you're hit by something such as divorce, illness, or loss of a job, it's going to hurt and it's going to take some time to get over it, even with God's help. But when discouragement comes your way, you can either fight against it, realizing that with God's help you're going to go on with your life, or you can give in to it and, literally or figuratively, take to bed and pull the covers over your head.

4. Have a proper perspective of time. Contemporary technology has given us a distorted picture of the world at two points. First, we tend to think that we can actually control the ultimate forces that shape life. Second, we assume that we can beat the clock. In both instances, we mistakenly believe that we can manipulate time.

As I mentioned earlier, ours has become the instant age. Microwaves and computers allow us to zip through life. A century ago our ancestors spent weeks—even months—traveling from coast to coast in covered wagons. Now we are able to fly completely around the world in less than a day. If you fly from Europe to the United States on the Concorde, you actually arrive here before you leave there because you're going faster than the time zones change. In a matter of seconds, we can fax a document to nearly any other country in the world.

And so all of these things have tended to distort our view of time. But time hasn't really changed. All that has changed is our perception of time. Sixty seconds is still a minute. Sixty minutes is still an hour. Twenty-four hours still makes up one day. The problem is that we are pushed to the limit to deal with all of the stimuli that are coming at us with rocket speed. It's easy to get caught up in the "information explosion" and rush around in a frenzy, rarely stopping to digest and reflect on the bits of data that continuously bombard us. But the truth is that now we need even more patience than at any time in the past.

Did you know that in spite of all the modern "labor-saving devices" most of us are actually working more hours per week than people did three to five decades ago? We must recover patience if we are going to endure and survive.

Do you ever feel as if you're rushing around like the proverbial chicken with its head cut off? If so, it's time to call a time-out. Stop the merry-go-round, get off, and catch your breath.

Maybe you'll want to get away for a couple of days—to the mountains, the beach, the desert, or anywhere else that's peaceful and will allow time for reflection. Then try to sort through your life. Are you overcommitted? What are you doing that isn't absolutely necessary? Where could you cut back? Be honest with yourself and then do your best to make the needed changes in your lifestyle.

It's an absolute necessity to call "time" every once in a while and reexamine your priorities and your commitments.

The Promises of Patience

We've already seen some of what the Bible has to say about patience, but there is a great deal more. One of my favorite passages is Psalm 37:

> Do not fret because of evil men
>   or be envious of those who do wrong;
> for like the grass they will soon wither,
>   like green plants they will soon die away.
>
> Trust in the LORD and do good;
>   dwell in the land and enjoy safe pasture.
> Delight yourself in the LORD
>   and he will give you the desires of your heart.
>
> Commit your way to the LORD;
>   trust in him and he will do this:
> He will make your righteousness shine like the dawn,
>   the justice of your cause like the noonday sun.
>
> Be still before the LORD and wait patiently for him;
>   do not fret when men succeed in their ways,
>   when they carry out their wicked schemes.
>   Psalm 37:1–7

The psalmist goes on to say in verses 18–19: "The days of the blameless are known to the LORD, and their inheritance will endure forever. In times of disaster they will not wither; in days of famine they will enjoy plenty." And in verse 25: "I was young and now I am old, yet I have never seen the righteous forsaken or their children begging bread."

This is a powerful passage full of fabulous promises from God to us. This is his commitment to us as individuals if we will do one thing: Wait patiently for him!

We Hate to Wait

It's not easy to wait.

Waiting is not the type of thing that brings us pleasure. No one has ever told me that one of their favorite pastimes was to wait.

Waiting aggravates us. It makes us angry, as this conversation illustrates: "Where were you? You said you'd be here at seven o'clock."

"Sorry. I got stuck in traffic."

"But it's 7:30. You know how I hate to wait."

Husbands are always complaining that their wives make them wait. You know the picture: While the wife is upstairs, hurriedly applying the finishing touches to her makeup, the husband paces back and forth in the living room, looking at his watch, shaking his head, wondering if she'll ever be ready to go. By the time she is ready to go, he'll be in such a bad mood from all that waiting that they might just as well stay home. The evening's going to be ruined anyway.

In case you think I'm picking on women, here's another scene that is replayed again and again in thousands of homes all across America. The wife has cooked a delicious dinner. She's spent hours in the kitchen sweating over a hot stove but it's been worth it because everything is perfect. The table is beautifully set. The food is steaming hot. All is ready.

"Honey, dinner's ready."

"Uh huh . . . just a moment."

A minute passes and he doesn't show up.

"Honey," she calls again, "come to the table."

"Yeah . . . yeah."

She can tell by the tone of his voice that he's making no move in the direction of the table. So she walks into the den to find his attention riveted on a basketball game on the tube.

Is she happy that he's made her wait? Of course not. Especially not when she thinks of all that food sitting on the table getting cold, just because her husband wanted to watch Michael Jordan "go to the hole."

It can just about drive you crazy when the doctor tells you that you'll have to wait two weeks to get the results of an important medical test.

People run up thousands of dollars in debts on their credit cards because they don't want to wait. Thirty or forty years ago people saved their money until they had enough to make a major purchase. Not anymore. Now, when you want a new TV or stereo or whatever, you just charge it or pay for it on the installment plan. Waiting is passé.

When you read what the Bible says about waiting on God, it sounds fine. *Sure, I can do that*, you think. But then when you realize what it means to wait, it's not so fine anymore.

I believe that our inability to wait has created tremendous problems in our society. People cut corners because they don't want to wait to do things right. People rob and steal because they don't want to wait for wealth to accumulate over time. Teenagers rush into premarital sex because they don't want to wait for marriage. Some people endanger themselves and others by driving too fast, simply because they can't wait to get to wherever it is they're going. Some people get themselves into terrible credit problems because they can't wait to have all the things they want. Many teenagers mortgage their futures by dropping out of school before they've graduated because they can't wait to get out into the world and start making money.

It's easy to see that all of this impatience results in plenty of trouble.

Godly Time Management

Everyone knows the old saying, "The best things in life are free." It's also true that "the best things in life take time."

If you've been injured in some way, it takes time for your body to heal. If you've been wounded by a broken relationship, it takes time for those emotions to heal. If there are hurts from your childhood that you've carried into your adult life, it takes time to deal properly with that pain. It takes time to develop lasting friendships, to build a marriage, to establish trust, to build a good reputation. It takes time to do just about anything that is truly worthwhile . . . such as waiting on the Lord.

It may increase your patience to realize that every minute you have is another gift from God. The minute you are living through right now, as you read the words I've written, is a gift from God. So when God tells you to wait for him, he is perfectly within his rights. He is asking you, in essence, to give back to him what he has already given you.

What we're talking about here is godly time management. I do not mean learning how to use your time more efficiently. I think it's good to know how to use your time wisely, and there are a number of courses and seminars you can take that will help you learn how to do that. But what I'm talking about goes much deeper. I'm talking about living patiently, waiting on the Lord, having an understanding of time that has everything to do with your wellness, your wholeness, your personal humanity, and your relationship with God.

This type of time management begins with an understanding of who God is: the Giver of time, the Giver of life, the Creator of all you see.

When God wrote the Ten Commandments on tablets of stone, the first one was "You shall have no other gods before me" (Exod. 20:3). Most of us know that commandment but we have a difficult time obeying it. When I put what I want ahead of what God wants, I'm making gods out of my desires and I'm living in disobedience to that commandment.

Many people go through life that way. They put their own agendas at the top of the list and do everything within their power to achieve their goals. Then, as time goes by and all those goals aren't met, life becomes more and more frustrating. After a time, they are tempted to alter their moral codes—to bend the rules a little bit—to get what they want out of life.

Am I talking about you? Actually, I'm talking about myself . . . or at least the way I used to be. There was a time when I truly believed that "the end justifies the means" when it came to achieving the goals I had set for myself. Today I am more of a "means" person than an "ends" person.

For example, I recently took my family on a trip to Montana to visit some friends. In the past I've always been extremely frustrated with the process of getting to the destination. Driving all the way from California to Montana would have been pure drudgery. I was concerned only with the ends and not the means.

But then God began to open my eyes to the beauty of his creation. This time, I thoroughly enjoyed the means, driving through the canyons and forests and stopping to see the historical markers on the way.

Because I took the time to savor the moment, I learned some things. For example, did you know that in 1910 a catastrophic fire burned three million acres of Northwestern forest? The smoke was so intense that it darkened skies as far away as London. I never would have known that if we had not stopped at one of those historical markers placed by the roadside. But because we stopped, we had the experience of learning about the horrendous fire and seeing the valley that had been dedicated to the memory of this cataclysmic event. Thus I began to understand the knowledge and beauty that can come to us if we are patient.

Taking the time to enjoy the moment does not mean that you have to forsake your goals. It does mean that you have to learn to be patient regarding the achieving of those goals.

My goal in this instance was to get my family to Montana. I didn't give up on that idea but I was patient as I moved toward its fulfillment.

Slow and Steady Does Win the Race

Every New Year's Day I sit down and write out a list of my goals for the year. I keep that list in a place where I can check it from time to time to make sure I'm heading in the right direction. But I understand that I'm not going to achieve everything on that list overnight.

I also have a list of more immediate things to do that I keep with me all the time. Sometimes it gets very long. That's okay because I don't let that list run my life. Instead, I use it to keep myself organized and on track. I understand now that the old fable about the tortoise and the hare is correct in its lesson that "slow and steady wins the race."

You see, everything does not have to happen "right now." It's okay to take your film to a place that will have your photos back to you the next day instead of in an hour. It's all right to take more than a minute to fix a cup of coffee. And it is certainly all right to wait on the Lord.

As you wait for the Lord to guide and direct you, you will see, experience, smell, taste, touch, and enjoy things that you would otherwise miss.

The world doesn't understand it, but there is joy in waiting. I can't begin to count how many informative articles I've read in my doctor's waiting room or all the interesting conversations I have had with people while I was waiting to board an airplane. So many times I've come up with ideas that have made my life better, simply because waiting gave me time to reflect.

Think One Hundred

I believe that most of the baby boomers are going to live to be over one hundred, if they can avoid any major accidents or illnesses.

If this sounds crazy, you should know that I'm basing my beliefs on several articles I've read. Life expectancies are increasing. There are already more than fifteen thousand people one hundred years old or older, so it is not that unusual anymore for someone to live that long.

What that means is that if you're forty years old, you've got another sixty years ahead of you. Think about what you could accomplish in that sixty years. Take money, for instance. If you put two thousand dollars per year into mutual funds and realize an annual growth rate of 10 percent, in forty years you will be a millionaire. That means you can rid yourself of any get-rich-quick dreams of winning the lottery and instead gain your wealth slowly, steadily, and surely, over time.

Maybe you won't live to be one hundred or more. But then again, maybe you will.

If you're thinking in those terms, then what's the rush? You've got time to do the things you want to do. More important, you have time to do the things God wants you to do.

Try asking him right now what he wants you to do today. Be patient and let him direct your steps.

You see, patience is not inactivity. It is, instead, passive action. Patience is taking the time to gain the necessary wisdom, guidance, and strength to take the actions God requires of you.

So have patience, wait on the Lord, and just watch the excitement begin to unfold.

7

Step Five
Kindness

... that best portion of a good man's life,
His little, nameless, unremembered acts
Of kindness and love.
                        William Wordsworth

You've probably heard this story dozens of times, but the beauty and truth it contains does not diminish over time.

A man was traveling on the road between Jerusalem and Jericho when he fell into the hands of robbers. Not only did they steal his money and his clothes, but they also beat him into unconsciousness and then left him to die.

A short while later a priest, a man of God, came walking along that same road and saw the injured man lying there. Instead of helping he crossed to the other side and continued on his way. He didn't want to get involved.

Pretty soon another man came by. He was a Levite, a devout, morally upright fellow. But he didn't want to be bothered either and so he too left the wounded man lying in the road, probably bleeding profusely, drawing closer to death every moment he went without medical attention.

Finally a Samaritan came by.

Now the Samaritans weren't anybody's favorite people—except, perhaps, of other Samaritans. They were a little bit rough around the edges. Unsophisticated. Hillbillies. If a Samaritan moved into your neighborhood, the property values were sure to take a tumble. They had too many kids. A lot of them were on welfare. Frankly, they had no class. At least, that's what the Jews thought of them.

But when the Samaritan saw the pathetic, crumpled figure in the roadway, he stopped to see what he could do to help. He wasn't carrying a first-aid kit but somehow he managed to bandage the fellow's wounds. Then, because there wasn't any hospital in the immediate vicinity, he took the man to a nearby hotel and spent the day nursing him back to health. He stayed by the stranger's side until he was sure the danger had passed and then paid the hotel manager to take care of him while he completed his trip, saying, "When I return I will reimburse you for any extra expense you may have" (Luke 10:35).

After Jesus told this story, he asked a question: "Which of these three do you think was a neighbor to the man who fell into the hands of robbers?" (v. 36).

The "expert in the law" who had been listening to Jesus' story gave the correct answer: "The one who had mercy on him."

"Go and do likewise," Jesus said (v. 37).

Jesus told this story nearly two thousand years ago. A lot of things have changed since then. We no longer travel long distances on foot or by riding donkeys, for instance. On the other hand, a lot of things have remained exactly the same. The human race has not progressed very far toward a moral utopia in the last two thousand years. This story has tremendous relevance for America in the 1990s.

It is relevant first of all because people are still being set upon by robbers and beaten and killed for no reason at all. We've all read stories about young men like Ennis Cosby who were shot and killed just because the attackers wanted their watch, shoes, or anything else they were wearing. That is a very sad commentary on modern society, and it shows what happens to morality when people are completely without kindness.

Jesus' story is also relevant because we have a lot of injured and battered people around us who need our help. Much of the time most of us go on about our business, intent on accomplishing the goals we have set for ourselves, and we pass these people by. Often it's not that we see them lying there wounded and cross to the other side of the street so we don't have to get involved. The truth is that we don't even see them!

Yet we encounter them every day, on the job, in our churches, at school. These are people who have been battered by the realities of life: a man who is lonely and feels that no one cares; a woman who has been abandoned by someone she loved and just needs someone to talk to; a child whose parents don't have time for her and who needs someone to show her that she's a worthwhile human being.

Such wounded, hurting people are all around us. They need a friendly touch, a kind word, a pat on the back, a little bit of encouragement so they can find the strength to keep going. All you have to do is ask God to open your eyes and fill your heart with kindness so you can react to them with love and compassion.

I am reminded of an old Winnie-the-Pooh story in which Eeyore, the donkey, has fallen into a river. Pooh comes along, sees him there, and engages him in conversation. First of all, Pooh asks if the river is cold. Why, yes, as a matter of fact it is.

Next, Pooh tells Eeyore that he really ought to be more careful. Yes, the donkey admits that it's true.

On further assessing the situation, Pooh has some news for his old friend. "I think you're sinking," he says.

And then, as Pooh prepares to go on his way, Eeyore humbly asks him, "If it's not too much trouble, would you mind rescuing me?"

Wow! Pooh never thought of that. Of course, he'd be more than happy to give his friend a hand.

You can find deep truths in some of the most unexpected places! Like Pooh, we all need to learn that when we see someone in trouble, the very best thing we can do is lend a helping hand.

Are You a Member of the Kindness Group?

Here's an interesting tidbit of information: The Greek word for "kindness" that is used in Galatians 5:22 is *chrestos*. The Greek word for "Christ" is *Christos*. In other words, there is a difference of only one letter between the word for Christ and the word for being kind to one another. Even though one word contains an *i* and the other an *e*, they were pronounced exactly the same.

Christians, of course, are followers of Christ. In the ancient Greek language, when you said you were a member of the Christian faith, you could actually also be saying that you were a member of "the kindness group." In other words, Christianity grew up with the whole concept of being kind to others.

Jesus taught that his followers should be kind to everyone they encountered. Through the parable of the Good Samaritan, he showed that he expects our kindness to extend to those who are far different from us.

He expects us to be kind to our enemies. He expects us to show kindness even to those who show by the way they live that they have no use for him.

Don't misunderstand. Being kind doesn't mean that you have to approve of everything another person does. That's not kindness at all. It is not kindness when you know that someone is engaging in destructive behavior but you refuse to speak to him or her about it.

When my wife and I were first dating, she gave me a copy of Khalil Gibran's *Sand and Foam*, and I found it to be an enjoyable and thought-provoking book. I remember especially one passage where he writes that he has learned silence from the talkative, tolerance from the intolerant, and kindness from the unkind.[1]

And yet, he says, he is not grateful to any of those teachers. When I read that, I determined that I would do my best to never show anyone what kindness is like by being unkind to them.

Demonstrating an Active Kindness

We have an obligation as people who believe in God to be kind to one another, to care for one another, to reach out and help one another. We are to demonstrate an active kindness that looks for ways to show the love of God to people in pain.

I recently read a story in the *Los Angeles Times* about a man who had been an executive with a motion picture company. He had a plush office in an elegant building but every day as he went to work, he was troubled by the poor and ragged people he passed on the streets—especially the children.

Just in case you've never been to Hollywood, I'll let you in on a little secret. It is not the most glamorous part of Los Angeles. I'm sure that a lot of tourists are quite surprised when they visit Hollywood for the first time. Yes, there are some movie studios there, some record companies, and some glamorous nightspots. And, yes, you might occasionally run into a movie star in one of the restaurants. But much of Hollywood is shabby—and I use that word kindly.

Hollywood has many sleazy bars and rundown nightclubs. It has lots of homeless people, including hundreds of teenagers who have come there looking for excitement and glamour but who have found quite the opposite.

They wind up sleeping on the streets, panhandling for money to buy food. Some go into prostitution. Many are addicted to drugs. Life is not pleasant for any of them.

The film company executive was so touched by the plight of these kids that he resigned his prestigious job and began a foundation to help them. These days he works long hours trying to get these kids off the streets and back into normal society.

He shelters, feeds, clothes, and counsels them. He tries to ensure that they finish high school and he offers them job training. He works fifteen and sixteen hours a day for about one third of the salary he used to make.

His help isn't always appreciated. He's got some great success stories to tell but he can also point to several young men and women who have gone right back to life on the streets despite everything he tried to do to help them. But he says he wouldn't think of giving up and going back to his old life, even though in many ways it was vastly more comfortable than the way he is living now.

Are you thinking, *He must be an amazing man?* I agree. But I also believe that he is demonstrating the sort of active kindness that God expects from all of us. I'm not suggesting that God expects you to quit your job and go into a full-time ministry or service of some kind. But I do mean that we should all actively look for opportunities to be kind.

If you have your eyes closed, you won't see people in trouble. If you stay comfortably in your own backyard, you aren't likely to encounter people who need your help.

I recently read another story in a local newspaper. A small group of special-education students from an elementary school were taken on a field trip to a mall as part of their "independence training." The children, all of whom have disabilities such as cerebral palsy, had gathered in their wheelchairs—where else?—in front of a toy store.

That's when a man came up, handed their teacher a one-hundred-dollar bill, and told her to let the kids get some toys. She tried to give the money back, but the man refused and quickly walked away.

The teacher was quoted as saying, "He didn't even tell me his name. I'd like to know so we could thank him." Can you imagine how much that act of kindness meant to those disabled kids?

You know, it really can be a lot of fun to "practice random acts of kindness and beauty" (as the bumper sticker says) and, as I said before, those acts don't have to take an extreme form like quitting your job to help the homeless or handing out hundred-dollar bills to children in shopping malls.

I remember one time during the Christmas holidays, for example, when my father and I were in Laguna Beach, California. Dad got a bunch of extra quarters and walked around town, putting them in parking meters that were about to run out of time. It was a simple gesture of kindness, a way to say,

"Merry Christmas" and "I don't want your day to be ruined by a parking ticket."

It wasn't the sort of thing that was going to turn the world upside down. But imagine how much better this world would be if we all looked out for each other that way—if we all did those little things to make other people's lives more pleasant.

I read somewhere about a woman who drove through a dollar tollbooth on her way to work one morning, handed the attendant ten dollars, and said, "This is for me and the next nine cars behind me."

The attendant shook his head and said, "Whatever you say."

That tollbooth attendant got some shocked looks from the next nine drivers when he told them, "Go on. Someone already paid for you." I'm sure those shocked looks quickly turned to smiles and I believe that the woman's simple act of kindness helped "make the day" for many of those harried commuters who benefitted from her generosity.

Taking a Personal Inventory

Are you kind? Really kind?

Most of us have learned how to act kindly, even though we may not really feel kind inside. We may express our sympathy to those who are hurting, pat them on the back, and tell them that things are bound to get better. But the kindness to which God calls us goes far beyond that. He calls us to a sincere kindness that often demands our time, our money, and our hearts.

Take a moment to think back to the Parable of the Good Samaritan, and then answer these questions.

1. Have you ever been a passerby in a similar situation? Or have you ever stopped to help when others were passing by? Think about why you reacted as you did and how you would act differently if the same situation arose today.
2. Which of the characters in Jesus' story do you most identify with? Why?
3. Has anyone been a "good Samaritan" in your life recently? What was it that person did to demonstrate kindness to you during a time when you were really hurting or in need? Why do you think that person responded to you as he or she did?
4. With which of the following responses are you most likely to react when someone comes up to you on a street corner and asks you for a handout?

- Ignore the person.
- Give the person money because you are embarrassed and want him or her to leave you alone.
- Try to find out what the person wants the money for before deciding if you will help.
- Assume that you're being conned and that whatever you give will probably go for drugs and alcohol.
- Offer to take the person to the grocery store or a restaurant and buy him or her something to eat.
- Come up with an excuse not to help.
- React in some other way.

Take another look at your list and see which of these responses clearly demonstrate godly kindness. How do you think God would want you to change your attitude and your behavior toward those in need?

5. Who do you think is more blessed by acts of kindness: the person giving or the person receiving? Why do you feel that way? Can you think of a personal experience that helped to shape your opinion?

6. Can you come up with a list of ten "little things" you can do to show kindness to your family members, friends, coworkers, and other acquaintances?

Developing Kindness

It isn't always easy to be kind. When you see someone in trouble it is much easier to hope that someone else will help the person than to help him or her yourself. But God wants to produce in you the fruit of kindness and he will if you will let him.

Ask God to help you and then try to step out in kindness to others. Before this day is over, look for at least one way to demonstrate kindness to someone in need.

Remember the words of Ella Wheeler Wilcox in her poem "The World's Need":

> So many gods, so many creeds,
> So many paths that wind and wind,
> While just the act of being kind
> Is all the sad world needs.

8

Step Six
Goodness

Waste no more time arguing what a good man should be. Be one.

Marcus Aurelius

Goodness is the antithesis of kindness.

When you were a child, did you ever try to build a house out of dominoes? Do you remember how frustrating that could be? You'd build it up to a certain level without any trouble, and then if you put one little domino just a bit too far to the right or the left, the whole thing would come tumbling down. Everything had to be balanced perfectly!

Devising a workable and proper system of personal morality can take every bit as much caution and precision as building a house with dominoes. Everything here has to be balanced perfectly too.

That's why I said that goodness is the antithesis of kindness.

Goodness is an understanding of what is right and proper. Goodness isn't always kind, and there comes a time when kindness must be given up for the sake of goodness. Jesus wasn't kind to the money changers when he drove them out of the temple with whips. But he was demonstrating goodness. Jesus certainly wasn't kind to the Pharisees when they were demonstrating arrogance and self-righteous ignorance of God's laws. When they deserved to be confronted, he confronted them. Again, Christ's actions may not have fit our definition of kindness, but he was definitely doing what was good.

Balance is always necessary.

For example, an overemphasis on love may lead you to lie down like a doormat and let other people walk all over you. That's not good for you or for them.

If you focus on joy to the neglect of the other fruit of the Spirit, you may move too far in the direction of self-love and self-indulgence. If you see peace as the primary building block of a system of personal morality, you are likely to develop a "peace-at-any-costs" attitude and you know what happened when Great Britain took that attitude with Germany during the 1930s.

What about patience? A wrong emphasis on patience will lead to procrastination and may stop you from taking action when you need to. In other words, someone may be engaging in a wrong activity—perhaps even abusing you—and you do nothing to stop it. But if instead you say, "Well, I've got to be patient, so I'll just wait and see what happens," you will let the abuse and the improper activity continue.

If you carry kindness to the extreme you become an enabler. An enabler is a person who helps someone else remain in dysfunctional or self-destructive behavior. For example, if you were married to an alcoholic, and he couldn't go to work because he had a hangover, you might think you were being kind if you called his boss and made an excuse for him. But that would be taking kindness to a harmful extreme, because it would allow your spouse's self-abusive and irresponsible behavior to continue.

Goodness Sets Necessary Limits

Look at it this way: Kindness produces the sort of response that is gentle and sweet; goodness must be added to kindness to set proper limits and to bring about correction when it is necessary.

If your kindness is not limited by an understanding of what is right and proper, it can move you into the realm of co-dependency and squeeze the life right out of you.

You may be co-dependent if

- you are so absorbed in other people's problems that you don't have time to identify or solve your own problems
- you care so deeply about other people that you have for-gotten how to take care of yourself
- you feel that you need to control events and people around you because it seems that everything is out of control
- you feel responsible for so much because you feel like other people in your life act responsibly for very little
- you have low self-esteem and thus believe you don't deserve to have good things happen to you

Goodness is an antidote to co-dependency because goodness frees you to love in a godly way . . . with healthy boundaries.

Let the Eagles Fly

Certainly it's important to be kind. It's important to lift one another up, to support one another, to encourage our broth-ers and sisters when we see that they need a kind word of encouragement. But there is a point when we need to allow the eagles to fly.

Consider how the mother eagle behaves as she builds her nest near the top of a tall tree or high up on the side of some mountain cliff. She lays her eggs in the nest and watches tenderly over them until they hatch. After that, she demonstrates the same devoted care to her little ones. She seems to spend nearly every waking moment caring for them. She feeds them. She keeps them warm. She flies into a rage to defend them at the slightest sign of danger.

Then the day comes when it is time for the eaglets to fly. What does that mother eagle do? She literally kicks the poor little guys out of their nest. She tosses them out into the blue and then it's "fly or else."

That doesn't seem like a very kind thing to do, does it? But they'd never learn to fly if their mother didn't take such drastic measures with them. They wouldn't be able to take care of themselves. They'd sit in that nest for the rest of their lives, content to let Mom spend her life waiting on them. Thus they would have completely wasted the potential that their Maker put within them—the potential to soar among the clouds.

The mother eagle's act in kicking her eaglets out of their nest may not be particularly kind but it is good and necessary and it sets a pretty good example for the rest of us.

Human parents could learn a thing or two from the mama eagle. Certainly it's important to care for our children, to protect them, and provide for their needs as long as they are incapable of caring for themselves. But when our children refuse to leave the nest, there comes a time when we must say, "You are now twenty-two years old. You are physically well. You are not mentally disabled. You need to be able to care for yourself."

It might be just about the hardest thing any parent has to say, but if your children don't seem inclined to fly off on their own, the day finally comes when you have to give them a forceful shove out into "the wild blue yonder."

It's not your responsibility to go out and find your son a job. It's not your responsibility to find your daughter an apartment. It's not your responsibility to give your children the financial resources they need to be on their own. You just need to give them a reasonable amount of time to figure out how they're going to support themselves. You could say, for example, "Son, this is your thirty-day notice. Thirty days from now, I expect you to have a job and be out on your own. Oh, and by the way, I'm converting your bedroom into an office."

Stop the Abuse

The goodness that sets limits is necessary in every type of relationship: in friendship, in romance, in interactions with your coworkers, and certainly in marriage.

Recently my children were watching a TV movie called "Radio Flyer," and I found myself getting interested. It's a cute fantasy about two little boys who in a desperate attempt to escape the wrath of their abusive, alcoholic stepfather build an airplane out of a little red wagon. The man's abuse is enabled by the boys' mother, a kindhearted woman who means well but who ultimately lets her sons down because she puts up with her husband's abuse.

At times she gets fed up and throws the man out of her house, but he always comes back crying, begging for one more chance, and promising that he's going to change his ways. Every time, she gives in.

For a very short while the stepfather keeps his word. Then he starts drinking, which makes him angry, and the beatings start all over again. So the little boys build an airplane to fly away from the abusive situation.

Of course this was only a movie. But you and I both know that there was nothing fictional about the cycle of abuse it portrayed. That type of thing is repeated over and over again in real life. Flesh-and-blood children are being abused every single day by one of their parents, and as in "Radio Flyer," the abuser is enabled to persist in his or her behavior by the other parent, who is too kind to take the action that would be necessary to stop it.

Real children can't escape such abuse by building an airplane out of a toy wagon and flying away.

A Time for Everything—Even Anger

Ecclesiastes 3:1 says, "There is a time for everything, and a season for every activity under heaven."

Surely there is a time for unbounded kindness, but there is also a time for goodness that holds people accountable for their actions. There is a time to draw the line, to set boundaries that you will not allow anyone to cross. You must learn to do this not only for your own sake, but for the sake of others as well.

There is also a time for anger.

That may surprise you. You may have been taught that anger is always wrong, that it's a sin. The Bible never says any such thing. It says that anger can cause you to sin if it's allowed to fester in your heart, because that's when it can ultimately cause you to engage in hurtful behavior toward another. But there is nothing at all wrong with anger that is properly handled. In fact I would go so far as to say that there are probably times when it's wrong not to get angry.

Do you remember what Moses did with the stone tablets on which God had written the Ten Commandments? You can find the story in chapters 32 through 34 of the Old Testament Book of Exodus.

Moses had gone up the mountain to commune with God and he wound up staying in God's presence for forty days. It was while he was there that God wrote the Ten Commandments on tablets of stone with his own finger.

It was also during that time that the people of Israel became restless waiting for Moses to return. Now, these people had seen for themselves the mighty miracles God had performed to bring them out of slavery in Egypt. They had looked on in awe as God brought ten terrible plagues on that nation, all in an effort to get Pharaoh to release the Israelites from their bondage. They had stood on the banks of the Red Sea and watched, mouths agape, as God rolled back the waves so they could cross safely on dry land, just ahead of the pursuing Egyptian army, and then they had seen those same waves crash back down on the heads of the pursuers, drowning them.

Yes, they had clearly seen God's hand at work. They had no reason to doubt that he was with them or that he would continue to lead them on to the Promised Land.

But when Moses didn't come back for forty days, they decided that something must have gone wrong. Perhaps he had fallen off a cliff or encountered a hungry mountain lion. The people came to Aaron, Moses' brother, and asked him to find a new god for them, a god they could see and bow down to. They weren't comfortable with an invisible God and they wanted to be able to worship something tangible. In response to their request, Aaron collected gold from the people, melted it down, and fashioned a golden calf, proclaiming it to be the god who had led them out of Egypt.

So after spending forty days with God and receiving the Ten Commandments, Moses came back down the mountain to find the people dancing and carrying on in front of the idol Aaron had made for them. Of course Moses was angry. He had good reason to be angry. He was so angry that he took those two stone tablets, on which was writing from God's own hand, and threw them to the ground, breaking them into pieces.

Think about it. Those tablets were unbelievably holy and sacred, but in his anger Moses destroyed them.

God never said a word to him about what he had done. God never chastised him and said, "Moses, you really need to control your temper." God understood that Moses' anger was righteous anger, and he simply prepared two more stone tablets and wrote the Ten Commandments all over again.

As this biblical account illustrates, there are times when anger is justified. It seems to me that there are times when it is sinful if we don't become angry, if we passively accept things we should never accept.

Are you angry when you read about innocent people who have fallen victim to the senseless violence that seems to permeate our society? Does it make you angry when you see violent criminals getting a light slap on the wrist from lenient judges?

Does it anger you to think about the millions of unborn children who are aborted every year? Does it make you angry when you turn on your television set during prime time and find yourself confronted by programs that glorify violence and casual sex and that depict those who believe in God as buffoons and morons?

All of those things make me angry, and I'm glad they do. I'd hate to be so desensitized that I took them all in stride.

I think we need to get mad enough to want to do something. Perhaps you remember the old movie *Network* and the line, "I'm mad as hell, and I'm not going to take it anymore!" Sometimes I'm surprised that I don't see more believers with that attitude! We need to get so angry that we decide we're not going to take it anymore.

We need to take a stand—for goodness.

Edmund Burke said, "The only thing necessary for evil to triumph is for good men to do nothing." How true that is. God calls us to do something, to act on behalf of goodness, and by his Spirit he gives us the power and strength we need to act in the ways he wants us to act.

Have you ever wondered what you would have done if you had been living in Germany prior to World War II? Think about it. As a German citizen, you would have had a pretty good life. The economy was moving along nicely. Hitler had cracked down on crime, so you could go out at night without fear of being robbed or mugged. The country seemed to be making its way back from the long, bleak, difficult years following World War I.

Would you have spoken out against the government's increasingly harsh policies against the Jews or would you have chosen to pretend that things were just fine?

You know, it's easy from the perspective of the 1990s to look back at the Germans of Hitler's day and wonder how the vast majority could have remained silent in face of the terrible things that were happening in their country, but sometimes I wonder. I'd like to think that I would have been on Dietrich Boenhoeffer's side, that I would have spoken out loudly and forcefully in behalf of goodness.

But then I look around at what's taking place in America today and wonder if I'm doing everything I possibly can to stand up for goodness in our society. Sometimes I have to ask myself, Is my lack of goodness allowing evil to gain the upper hand here? Is my "kindness" borne out of strength—or weakness?

We Have the Answer

Those of us who believe in God ought to be operating from a position of strength and power. I'm afraid that instead we are too often weak and fearful.

We should be strong because we understand the power that created this world and everything in it. We should be powerful because we have God's Spirit to protect and guide us. When we look around and see our society crumbling in so many ways, we ought to be able to do more than just shake our heads and say, "That's really a shame." We have the answer that will remedy society's ills, and that answer is God's love. It's up to us to take that answer out into a needy world. We have the power to bring about lasting change in our world because God gives us that power.

Billy Graham writes:

> The word "good" in the language of Scripture literally means "to be like God," because He alone is the One who is perfectly good. It is one thing, however, to have high ethical standards but quite another for the Holy Spirit to produce the goodness that has its depths in the Godhead. The meaning here is more than just "doing good." Goodness goes far deeper. Goodness is love in action. It carries with it not only the idea of righteousness imputed, but righteousness demonstrated in everyday living by the Holy Spirit. It is doing good out of a good heart, to please God, without expecting medals and rewards. Christ wants this kind of goodness to be the way of life for every Christian. Man can find no substitute for goodness, and no spiritual touch-up artist can imitate it.[1]

Writing recently in *Christianity Today*, Chuck Colson talks about a press conference President Clinton had on MTV. Most of the press conference was given over to what you might expect on MTV—questions about the President's taste in clothes and such. Then a seventeen-year-old girl named Dahlia Switzer had a far more serious question: "Mr. President," she said, "it seems to me that singer Curt Cobain's recent suicide exemplified the emptiness that many in our generation feel. How do you propose to teach our youth how important life is?"

In response to this difficult question, Colson writes:

> The real message of Dahlia's question is that the reigning orthodoxy of secularism is crumbling. By rejecting any transcendent world, secularism abandoned people to try to find happiness solely in this world. In making money and buying things. As Jesus warned, we are easily consumed by worldly concerns. What to eat, and what to wear.
>
> His words were prophetic in secular, consumer America. Our public life has been stripped of abstract ideas like the true and the good, leaving us wandering in the desert of our own desires. Unchecked desires lead straight to family breakdowns, social disarray, and crime.
>
> Today, social decay is creating a deeper hunger for moral truth. Christianity can fill that hunger. We can simply present the facts. The statistics show that Christian marriages are stronger, that kids raised in the church are more likely to resist sex and drugs. Crime recedes when spiritual values are ascended. If we want to address Dahlia Switzer among our young people, if we want to address the millions who tell pollsters they're yearning for something deeper, then we must give them what only the church can give: A message of truth and meaning based on the one who is truth.[2]

A recent poll taken by the *Times/Mirror* news group found that 71 percent of Americans are dissatisfied with the way things are going in the country today. *Newsweek* found that

76 percent of Americans believe the country is in moral and spiritual decline.

Why do people feel this way? It's not what you might think. People aren't upset about the economy or the tax rates. They are worried, instead, about rising crime rates and other social issues.

They are distressed by the lack of goodness in our society.

How Do You Rate in Goodness?

Do you have true goodness, what Billy Graham calls "love in action"? Ask yourself these questions to find out.

1. Can you think of a recent occasion when you were able to use anger constructively to say no to something wrong that was being done? If so, think about why you did what you did and how you felt afterward.
2. Can you think of any situations in your life at present where you have been kind for far too long and ought to set some limits? If so, how are you going to change that situation?
3. Can you think of ways in which you have enabled other people to abuse you or continue wrongful behavior? If so, what do you need to do to stop enabling other people?
4. What do you think "tough love" looks like? Are there areas in your life where you need to show "tough love"?

Our society is desperate for goodness, and only those of us who believe in God understand what goodness really is.

9

Step Seven
Faithfulness

O heaven! were man
but constant, he were perfect.
Shakespeare

I was flipping channels the other night and came across one
of those rather unsavory "real life" television talk shows.

I don't normally watch those programs. In fact I have very
little time for watching television at all. But for some reason,
this show caught my attention. It was a little bit like what
happens when you're driving along the freeway and come on
an accident. You don't really want to look but you're curious
and you find yourself rubbernecking right along with all your
fellow travelers.

So I stopped for a few minutes, morbid curiosity getting the
best of me, to see what the hot topic of discussion was on this
particular night. There was a woman on the show—not a particularly attractive woman to be sure—who said she was making a great deal of money "investigating" husbands to see if
they were faithful.

She was hired by women who suspected that their husband was unfaithful or who at least thought that their husband had a roving eye. They'd arrange for this woman to "accidentally" meet up with their husband somewhere, where she'd flirt with them and, basically, try to seduce them. If the husband went for the "bait," she'd take the evidence back to the wife, and the result would be one more happy divorce lawyer.

From the way this woman told her story, she was rarely turned down. She obviously didn't think much of men in general and felt that most members of the gender aren't the slightest bit interested in being faithful to their wives.

I hope she's wrong about that. I hope she's not telling the truth. Like I said, this woman was no latter-day version of Helen of Troy. But I'd like to think that even if she were a "perfect 10" the vast majority of married men would still choose to be faithful to their wives.

I know there are faithful people in this world; I encounter them every day. I know a man who has been married to the same woman for more than fifty years and he still loves her dearly. He shows how much he loves her by sitting with her at the table and feeding her, as if she were a baby, because she can no longer feed herself. She makes a terrible mess. He doesn't seem to mind.

Sometimes she is afraid and cries. He calms her by kissing her cheek and telling her how much he loves her. Occasionally she gets angry for no reason at all. Again, he does whatever he can to comfort her.

He helps her get dressed every morning. He brushes her hair and tells her how beautiful she is and that she'll always be the love of his life. He bathes her. He even changes her diapers.

She never says a word of thanks. The truth is that she doesn't even know he's there. She's in the final stages of Alzheimer's. She has left the world of reality behind.

For the past several months she has been living in a world that ceased to exist many years ago. She talks to friends she hasn't seen since she was a girl. She plays with her sister who died ten years ago.

You might think her husband would give up. After all, he's not a young man and caring for his wife in this way takes its toll. But he insists that he will personally care for her as long as he is physically and financially able.

He does it because he loves her. You can see it in the tender and gentle way he cares for her. Because he loves her, he is going to be faithful, no matter what.

I know he's not the only one so committed. There are thousands of others in our society who demonstrate the same level of faithfulness, in many different ways, on a daily basis. But no matter how many such people there may be, we need more of them.

Unfortunately our society doesn't seem to put a very high premium on faithfulness in romantic love or any other area of life. Movies, TV, and books all bombard us with the idea that only "squares" are faithful, and that's a shame, because faithfulness is one of the primary building blocks of a just and moral society.

God Is Faithful

Faithfulness is the seventh fruit of the Spirit listed in the fifth chapter of Galatians—a gift to his people from a faithful God.

God, in fact, is the perfect example of faithfulness. He says to us: "Never will I leave you; never will I forsake you" (Heb. 13:5). Revelation 19:11 calls God he who is "Faithful and True."

The entire Bible is a testimony to God's faithfulness. The Old Testament is an account of God's faithfulness and loyalty to his people despite their frequent infidelities. In the New Testament, the life of Christ emphasizes the theme of God's faithful love for a people who don't seem much interested in loving him back.

The ache in God's broken, betrayed heart can be felt in Jesus' anguished words: "O Jerusalem, Jerusalem, you who kill the prophets and stone those sent to you, how often I have longed to gather your children together, as a hen gathers her chicks under her wings, but you were not willing" (Luke 13:34). What a poignant view of the faithfulness of God!

Abraham: A Great Example of Faith(fulness)

What do you think of when you consider the word "faithfulness"? Do you think of being "full of faith" or of being "trustworthy and reliable"? Actually faithfulness is both qualities. You can't have one without the other. As with the other virtues we have been studying, faithfulness is a gift from God, given to help us live moral, happy lives.

To understand faithfulness, it is necessary to take a close look at faith. What is faith? It is a total willingness to do whatever God wants you to do. Hebrews 11:6 tells us that "without faith it is impossible to please God," and Ephesians 2:8 says that faith "is the gift of God."

So God gives his people a certain amount of faith and then he expects them to increase it through a continual process of trusting in him. Like a tiny seed, if it is planted and watered properly, a small amount of faith in God will take root and begin to grow. The growth will not be visible at first, because it will be taking place deep below the surface as roots are spreading out and forming an anchor that will not give way in the storms of life.

Although each change will be gradual and almost imperceptible, soon this faith will be so strong and powerful that it will be able to move mountains (see Matt. 17:20). Can you see, then, how faith leads to faithfulness?

One of the best examples of this kind of faith is the Old Testament hero Abraham. Abraham never doubted that God would fulfill his promise to make him a father of many nations, even though he and his wife, Sarah, were well into old age when God made this promise to them.

Abraham's life was marked by mistakes, sins, and failures as well as by wisdom and goodness. In everything he did, he consistently trusted God. His life is a prime example of faith in action. If he had looked only at his own abilities, he would have decided that it was impossible for him to become the father of anyone, much less a mighty nation. But instead of looking to himself, he looked to God, believed him, and waited for him to fulfill his promise.

In the fourth chapter of Romans the apostle Paul writes:

What does the Scripture say? "Abraham believed God, and it was credited to him as righteousness."

Against all hope, Abraham in hope believed and so became the father of many nations, just as it had been said to him, "So shall your offspring be." Without weakening in his faith, he faced the fact that his body was as good as dead—since he was about a hundred years old—and that Sarah's womb was also dead. Yet he did not waver through unbelief regarding the promise of God, but was strengthened in his faith and gave glory to God, being fully persuaded that God had power to do what he had promised. This is why "it was credited to him as righteousness." The words "it was credited to him" were not written for him alone, but also for us, to whom God will credit righteousness—for us who believe in him who raised Jesus our Lord from the dead. He was delivered over to death for our sins and was raised to life for our justification.

Therefore, since we have been justified through faith, we have peace with God through our Lord Jesus Christ.

Romans 4:3, 18–5:1

Humanly speaking, there was no hope that Abraham and Sarah would ever have a child. But God, responding to Abraham's faith, empowered Sarah and him physically so they were able to give birth to Isaac, the child of promise, the one through whom the Messiah would come.

Faith was of constant importance in Abraham's life, as it is in ours. The first steps of faith led to further steps, until finally the ultimate test came and God commanded him to sacrifice Isaac on an altar. Faith enabled Abraham to take even this startling command in stride without losing confidence in God. He obeyed here as in every other area of life.

We too can trust God this much. When we understand that he is totally trustworthy, even the most difficult steps of obedience become possible.

The more God touches our lives with his love and grace, the more full of faith we become. And the more full of faith we are, the more the fruit of faithfulness will be evident in our lives.

God's View of Faithfulness

Faithfulness is always honored by God. In Matthew 25:21 Jesus says that the person who is faithful in a few things will be put in charge of many things. Revelation 2:10 says, "Be faithful, even to the point of death, and I will give you the crown of life."

We can see that God puts a very high premium on faithfulness. Yet the question remains, What does it mean to be faithful?

The answer is that a faithful person is trustworthy and loyal. Being faithful involves doing what you said you were going to do.

A faithful spouse is one who means what he or she says in the wedding vows when he or she promises to "forsake all others." A faithful friend is one with whom you can share any confidence and know that your trust will not be betrayed. A faithful employee is one you can count on to give you an honest day's work for a day's pay.

A faithful employer is one you can count on to give you an honest day's pay for a day's work. Dennis Washington became the success he is because he understood this principle. In 1995 Dennis Washington was inducted into the Horatio Alger Association, a group comprised of people who have succeeded in spite of incredible odds against them.

Washington was raised in Montana by various relatives. After graduating from high school, he moved to Alaska and worked for a heavy construction company. A few years later he moved back to Montana. At the age of twenty-nine he borrowed thirty thousand dollars and went into business for himself. He was quite successful, but his big break came when he had the opportunity to buy the Anaconda Copper Mine in Butte, Montana.

The mine workers, represented by thirteen different unions, had been on strike for three years. The effect on the community was devastating. With that many unions, settlement was unlikely. Because there was plenty of ore, Washington knew that if he could create peace everyone could go back to work.

Coming up with a solution that would be fair to him and to his employees, he proposed that his employees accept low salaries—which was necessary to operate the mine in the black—and he would give them a share of the mine's profits. The employees accepted the proposal, and five years later they were the highest paid mine workers in the world.

Today Washington is recognized as the father of modern profit sharing. As a result of his willingness to give an honest day's pay for an honest day's work, he is one of America's wealthiest men.

It will always be true that making a profit is important. Any company that fails to make a profit can't stay in business. At the same time, many companies need to have a sense of loyalty to their employees.

Needed: An Honest Society

To be faithful is to be honest, without deceit. That is another area in which our society could use some improvement.

The *Reader's Digest* recently checked out the honesty factor in several American cities by planting a number of "lost" wallets with one hundred dollars in them.[1] In addition to the money, each of the wallets contained "the owner's" identification and some photos from his family. Anyone who wanted to find the owner could do it with a simple phone call. Those wallets were dropped on streets in cities of various sizes, and then the *Digest* writers sat back and waited to see what would happen.

It may surprise you to know that a few more than half of the wallets were returned. As you might expect, far more of the wallets were returned in smaller cities. As you might not expect, the people who picked up the wallets and failed to return them were not necessarily the ones who seemed to need money. *Digest* researchers told of watching as a woman got out of a late-model luxury car, picked up one of the wallets, and stuffed it into her pocket. She never turned it in.

On the other hand, they saw a wallet being picked up by a homeless man. They could tell that he didn't have any money, so they figured they'd never see that wallet again. But the homeless fellow surprised them by heading straight for the nearest police station and turning it in.

So the news is not all bad. There are honest people out there, and they are not always who you think they are. But you already knew that.

Now think how much better off this world would be if the vast majority of us demonstrated that sort of honesty and faithfulness. It's easy to see that faithfulness ought to be an important ingredient in your moral code.

You Can't Please Everyone!

In faithfulness, as in every other trait we're discussing in this book, balance is necessary. The person who tries to be faithful to everyone often ends up being faithful to no one—least of all himself.

I can explain that best by using myself as an example. I have four children. I want to be faithful to all of them. I also have a wife, and of course I want to be faithful to her. I have parents, and I want to be faithful to them. Then there are all the other members of our family: a dog, a bunny, a bird, a hamster, and a goldfish.

You can see that I have quite a few obligations. What happens if I forget to be faithful to one of them? Suppose I forget to feed the goldfish. He'll die. Or suppose I forget to be faithful to the dog by putting him on his leash, and he runs into the street and gets hit by a car.

What if all of my children want me to be faithful to them by attending functions on the same night at the same time? Well, I just can't do that! There's no way I can be in four places at once, without being torn into four pieces or having three clones made.

That's a pretty good picture of what happens to the person who tries to be faithful to too many people at once. We all want to be faithful to our families, to our church, to God, to other people, to our work, and so on. But there have been times in my life when I wanted to scream because I could not possibly do everything for everybody else.

Because you can't be faithful to everyone, you have to set some boundaries. You do that by deciding what your priorities are, determining what you will and won't do, and then abiding by the decisions you've made. Establishing proper boundaries will keep you from getting sucked into things you really don't want to get sucked into and prevent you from making commitments and promises when you really don't want to.

It's important to be faithful, yes, but it's also important not to get so overcommitted that you're of no use to anyone. That's precisely what will happen if you don't learn a very important word: no.

That little word is vital to your mental health, and if it's not a regular part of your vocabulary, it should be. You can use it like this: "No, I'm sorry, I can't do that"; "No, I can't be there because I have another commitment at that time"; "No, I really can't help you. You'll have to find someone else."

Some people don't have any trouble at all saying no. For others, it takes a real effort because they want everybody to like them. But no matter what you do, you're never going to get everybody to like you. It's just impossible.

The Bible has some harsh words about those who love "the praise of men" (John 12:43).

A friend told me how mad she was at herself when she discovered the lengths to which she would go to get someone to like her. It happened when she was out of town on a business trip, went out to an expensive restaurant for dinner, and wound up with a waiter who was rude to the point of being insulting. Despite the waiter's attitude, when the check came, she dutifully left a tip worth 15 percent of the total bill.

Later on when she thought about it, she realized what she'd done. She had left her customary tip because she wanted the waiter to think well of her, to like her. Why? He wasn't a particularly nice person. In fact he had acted pretty much like a jerk the entire evening. Besides, she'd never eaten in that restaurant before. Chances were pretty good she would never eat there again. That meant she'd probably never see that particular waiter again, so why did it matter what he thought of her?

The truth was that it didn't. She learned an important lesson that day about setting boundaries, about saying no, about the fact that some people simply aren't going to like you no matter what you do. She learned that more important, it's not worth it to have some people like you.

It's important to know that God approves of you, and to be certain of that it's necessary to be faithful to him. It's very important that you like yourself, so you need to be faithful to you. After that, you need to decide who deserves your faithfulness. Most likely it will be the members of your immediate family, your friends, your coworkers, and people in your neighborhood. Even here you should have clear priorities and stick to them.

Setting Up Your Boundaries

It's up to you to decide how you will set up your boundaries and once you have decided what they are to make decisions accordingly.

I have set up my own boundaries according to five distinct priorities:

1. God
2. myself
3. my family
4. my job
5. my friends and other people

Your priorities do not have to be the same as mine. What matters is that you have given serious thought to what things are most important to you. Doing so will help you manage your life and avoid being pulled in too many different directions at once. To help you set your own priorities, I want to tell you how I came up with mine.

1. My first priority in faithfulness is God. I put God first in my life for a whole host of reasons.

One of those reasons is that he made me. That means he understands me better than anyone else, which means he knows what is best for me. I can never go wrong doing what God wants me to do. Keeping him as my first priority in life prevents me from making mistakes based on my own selfishness or based on the selfishness of others who might want to control me.

Also, because God created me, I owe him everything, including my existence. Therefore it's only right that I should put him first on my list of areas in which I resolve to be faithful.

Another reason why God is my first priority is that I want to live in paradise, not only in this life but also in the life after this life. I believe that putting God before anything else ensures that this will happen. God gives meaning to my life here on this earth, and he also promises me that when I die he will take me home to live with him forever in a land full of the grace, joy, wonder, and splendor of his presence.

Eternal life doesn't begin when you die. It begins the moment you allow the Spirit of God to enter your heart and start growing his fruit in your life—the love, joy, peace, patience, and so on that we have been talking about. As you experience these virtues and gifts, you will begin living in paradise.

Paradise begins now and continues after death. I would go so far as to say that if you are not happy in life today, there's a good chance you're not going to be happy with the way things are after you die. So if you find that you're not happy, perhaps it's because you're not fully surrendered to God, because you have not yet yielded your life to his Spirit and cooperated with him to produce the fruit of the Spirit in your life.

You know, faith in God is like a perpetual motion machine. For centuries scientists and inventors tried to come up with a machine that would produce as much energy as it used up. Think about it: You'd turn it on once and it would run forever. No batteries needed. No electrical outlet required. It would just go on and on and on doing its work . . . forever.

Unfortunately nobody has ever been able to come up with a machine like that. But that's precisely how faith works.

When you make a decision to have faith in God, when you allow his Spirit control over your life, he begins to impart more faith to you. The more you use the faith he gives you, the more he gives you. You will never use it up but will only obtain more of it, with the result that your life will be a happy, exciting adventure.

Another reason why God is my first priority is that the Bible tells me that's what he expects. As we've discussed before, the second of the Ten Commandments is "You shall have no other gods before me" (Exod. 20:3).

When Jesus was asked to name the greatest commandment, he answered, "Love the Lord your God with all your heart and with all your soul and with all your mind" (Matt. 22:37). He also said, "Do not worry, saying, 'What shall we eat?' or 'What shall we drink?' or 'What shall we wear?' For the pagans run after all these things, and your heavenly Father knows that you need them. But seek first his kingdom and his righteousness, and all these things will be given to you as well" (Matt. 6:31–33).

For all these reasons, I have resolved to be faithful to God.

2. My second priority in faithfulness is myself. At first glance that may sound selfish, but it's really not.

Have you ever known anyone who gave and gave and gave until he or she just couldn't give anymore? I think of mothers who are trying to raise a couple of kids, holding down a full-time job, and struggling to keep on top of things financially. As if that's not enough, they volunteer to be room-mothers, Sunday school teachers, or anything else until there is *nothing* left for their own spiritual growth and development.

If a mother doesn't put her own well-being first, she's bound to self-destruct. She won't have anything left to give her kids, and the entire family will suffer.

I also know of many clergymen who have run themselves into the ground trying to take care of all the church business. They run and run on that treadmill, until the day finally comes when they hit the wall. They fall to the ground exhausted, and they simply can't go on.

You cannot give to others unless you give to yourself. That is precisely why I make sure I'm faithful to myself. What good is a sick dad going to be for his kids? I'm not going to be any good to them if I'm not healthy emotionally, spiritually, and physically. I won't be able to meet my wife's needs if I've run myself into the ground. Nor will I be of much use to God. I have to take care of myself so that I'm able to do what he wants me to do with my life.

Read through the New Testament and you'll find that Christ often went off alone to pray. He needed time away from the crowds that constantly surrounded him; he needed to get away so he could have his own soul restored.

As I said before, your priorities for faithfulness may not be exactly the same as mine, but you do need to rank high on your list. So take care of yourself. Get proper amounts of rest and relaxation. See to it that you get enough exercise. Make sure you get enough sleep every night. Eat properly. Tend to your own needs. There are people who love you, who are depending on you, and who need you to take care of yourself for their sake.

Shakespeare put it this way in *Hamlet:*

> This above all: to thine own self be true.
> And it must follow, as the night of the day,
> Thou canst not then be false to any man.

A smart fellow, that Shakespeare.

3. *My third priority in faithfulness is my family.* Because my family is important to me, the needs of my spouse and children must take precedence over the needs of others. Thus, if I'm forced to choose between being faithful to my family or

being faithful to my job or my friends, I'm going to choose my family.

I believe there are a number of specific ways you can demonstrate faithfulness to your family every single day. For example, if you are married, it's important to demonstrate your faithfulness to your husband or wife by spending time with him or her. I believe that every married couple should set aside one night a week for dating—for being together without the kids or anyone else.

It doesn't really have to be a dinner-and-dancing type of date. It might involve shipping the kids off to a relative's house for the evening so you can have the house to yourselves for a while. You might want to take a walk in the park or go for a drive in the country. The important thing is that it's time set aside for just the two of you, time when you can talk about what's on your minds and grow closer in your relationship.

I also believe that every husband and wife should spend some quality time with each other every day, even if it's over the phone. It's important to share the events of the day with each other, to plan together and talk about the issues that are facing you as a couple. It's important for every married couple to laugh, cry, and dream together as often as possible.

It's also important for parents to spend time with their children. Children need your love and your guidance. They need to be able to talk to you about their hopes and dreams as well as their fears and problems. They need to know that you are going to be there for them and that you take their feelings and their wishes seriously.

I realize that you can't always base your decisions on what your children want or need. If you are a businessman who travels a great deal, you can't always be present at Little League games, school awards assemblies, and such. But you can see to it that you attend one a week or one a month. Set a measurable goal and attain it.

If you can't be there on an occasion that is important to your child, you can take the time to explain why. The child may not be able to understand right now why you can't be there, but in the long run, he or she will come to understand and appreciate the fact that you cared enough to explain.

Even when you are making a decision that seems to be a matter of job versus family, it's important to keep a balance. For example, your job is the means by which you provide for your family. Thus if your job demands excessive hours from you or takes you away from home for long periods but is the only way you have to support your family, then you're demonstrating faithfulness to your family by working all those hours or spending all that time on the road.

If, on the other hand, you are the one who makes the decision to work all those hours and do all that traveling, then you're not demonstrating faithfulness to your family. If you spend very little time with your spouse and children because you've made a decision to work, if you are constantly missing important events in the life of your children, then I suggest that you reconsider your priorities in life.

4. *My fourth priority in faithfulness is my job.* In my case, my fourth and fifth priorities are completely intertwined. That's because my job is to serve as pastor of Rancho Capistrano Community Church, and many of my friends are members of that church. Being faithful in my job as a pastor also ties in to faithfulness with my friends.

Some people have come to believe that work is a curse—that it's something people have to do but don't really enjoy. They are wrong.

Others think of work as the centerpiece of their lives. They have come to define themselves by what they do for a living. They too are wrong. That view leads toward workaholic behavior, which can be just as destructive as alcoholism or any other addiction.

The truth about work is that it is ordained by God, something he has expected us to do since the beginning of creation. Work is part of what gives us value as human beings, but only part.

If you go back to the very beginning of the Bible and read the second chapter of Genesis, you'll find that after God created the first man, one of the very next things he did was give him a job: "The LORD God took the man and put him in the Garden of Eden to work it and take care of it" (Gen. 2:15).

You know we live in a world that isn't quite the way God intended it to be. It has been corrupted by sin, which brought death, decay, and all sorts of horrible things into life on this planet. But sin has nothing to do with work. Work was here long before sin ever entered the picture.

Work, in fact, is one of the ways God chooses to bless us— one of the ways he gives us the necessities of life. It is one of the ways by which he gives us the means to help the poor: "He who has been stealing must steal no longer, but must work, doing something useful with his own hands, that he may have something to share with those in need" (Eph. 4:28).

Work is also something that brings respect: "Make it your ambition to lead a quiet life, to mind your own business and to work with your hands, just as we told you, so that your daily life may win the respect of outsiders and so that you will not be dependent on anybody" (1 Thess. 4:11).

God could choose to take care of you by giving you everything you need on a daily basis. If he wanted to, he could even drop manna out of the sky onto your front lawn every morning. But like those little eaglets we talked about earlier, you would never be able to develop your full potential, and it is important to God that you do so.

I think of the children of Israel, who were in the wilderness for forty years after leaving the slavery of Egypt behind them. They were on their way to a Promised Land that was flowing with milk and honey but because they were disobedient to God, it took them a long, long time to complete their journey.

As tough as life in the wilderness may have been, they had very little work to do while they were there. God provided food by sending manna from heaven or by driving game into their midst. When they were thirsty he provided water from a rock. He blessed their clothes so that they never wore out. He took care of them in every possible way.

Still, they weren't happy out there in the wilderness. They longed for the Promised Land and for the "milk and honey" they would find there.

When they were finally allowed to enter that glorious country, that's when they had to start working. They had to clear the land. They had to plant crops. They had to milk their cows and goats to get that milk. They had to go out and gather the honey.

We tend to think sometimes that there won't be any work in the Promised Land, but I'm convinced that the opposite is true. There is plenty of work in paradise, but it is the sort of work that brings fulfillment and joy.

It will be the type of work Solomon was talking about when he wrote: "I saw that there is nothing better for a man than to enjoy his work" (Eccles. 3:22). Work is a high-priority item with God, and it ought to be a high-priority item with you and me as well.

So wherever you put work on your list of life's priorities, remember that it's important to be faithful on your job. What that means is that you

- are honest with your employer, giving an honest day's work for an honest day's pay
- do not take anything from your employer without permission—stationery, long-distance telephone calls, or supplies
- do not call in sick unless you really are sick
- do your fair share of the work so that others don't have to carry more than their share of the workload

I know that you already know all of these things, but sometimes we have a tendency to forget how important faithfulness on the job really is, how vital the little things can be. As for me, I certainly wouldn't want to fly on an airplane on which the mechanics weren't faithful to the job that was entrusted to them.

We all know of disasters or near disasters that have occurred because some worker somewhere decided to cut corners or because he or she wasn't paying attention at a critical moment. That person wasn't faithful to the job entrusted to his or her care, and the result was catastrophic.

We hear a lot of talk these days about how products made in other countries are superior to products made here in the United States. I'm not sure that's true, because I believe in the American worker. However, if we are ever going to regain our position as the world's top manufacturing nation, we will have to understand the importance of faithfulness on the job.

5. My fifth priority in faithfulness is my friends and other people. The fact that friends and other people come last on my list of priorities doesn't mean that I don't value my friends or that I don't think other people are important. What it means is that there are other parts of my life that have to come first.

It's only because I know what my priorities are that I can make proper decisions as to how I spend my time. For instance, if a friend or neighbor calls on me to do something for him, I ask myself the following questions:

- Will it interfere with my faithfulness to God?
- Will it interfere with my faithfulness to myself?
- Will it interfere with my faithfulness to my family?
- Will it interfere with my faithfulness to my job?

If the answer to all of those questions is no, then I am free to fulfill the request from my friend or neighbor. If I can see that fulfilling the request being made of me will cause me to be less than faithful in one or more of these other areas, then I say, "No, I can't do that."

I don't have to give an explanation if I don't want to. I just say no and let that be good enough.

Of course I'm not talking about an emergency situation. If my neighbor needs me to help him out in an emergency, of course I will.

It's not usually emergencies that steal our time from us and cause us to become overly committed and stressed out. Instead, it's almost always the little things that crowd in on us until we can hardly breathe.

Preparing a Time Budget

Once you have established what your priorities are, it might help you to keep a journal for a couple of weeks to find out how you are really spending your time. Keep a daily record of how much time you spend with God, with yourself, with your family, and so on. You may be surprised by what you find out. For example, you may find that even though you think your family is high on your list of priorities, the truth is that you're really spending very little time with them. You may even find that you're not really taking any time at all for yourself.

Once you've kept that journal for a couple of weeks and can see clearly how you are really spending your time, then draw up a list of how you'd *like* to spend your time. How much time do you want to spend with God—in Bible study, in worship services, just communing with him one to one? How much time would you like to have for yourself? for your family? for the other priorities in your life?

What I'm suggesting, really, is that you might want to start budgeting your time in much the same way as you budget your money. Start with the reality that there are 168 hours in a week and that a big chunk of those are spent sleeping. If you sleep an average of seven hours per night, that's forty-nine hours weekly.

How do you want to spend the hours that are left to you? Some of those hours will be spent working, eating, bathing, traveling to and from work, and taking care of other personal necessities. When you get right down to it, you're probably going to find out that you don't have as many hours as you thought you did in which to do the things you want to do.

If you're like most of the people I know, you're probably going to look at your time budget and say, "No wonder I feel stressed out all the time!"

This is when you start budgeting your time, eliminating from your schedule things you really don't want or need to do and adding things that are more important, such as time for yourself and your family. In that way you can be faithful in the areas where you need to be faithful and you can have a life that is ordered and peaceful rather than frenetic and out of control.

When you are carefully budgeting your time, you may find that your faithfulness to others is actually increasing instead of decreasing. It is more faithful to others to say, "No, I'm sorry, I really don't have the time for that" than to say yes to something you really don't have the time or the heart to do. Better to say no in the first place than to do a shoddy or half-hearted job.

Pursuing Faithfulness

To help yourself grow stronger in faithfulness, ask yourself the following questions:

1. Have you ever gotten sucked into doing something you didn't want to do? What was it? How did you feel after agreeing to do it? What will you do to avoid such a situation in the future?
2. What do you think of when the word "faithful" is mentioned? Do you see yourself as being faithful? Are there times when you fall short in this area? If so, why?
3. Has there been a time recently when you were struggling to be faithful to several people who were pulling

you in different directions? If so, how did you resolve this conflict?

4. Have you established definite boundaries in your life? Do you struggle with recognizing your own limitations? Do you overspend, overwork, overcommit, or overcare?

5. Do you ever avoid making decisions because you don't want to have to choose between one thing and another? Can you think of some times when indecision has caused problems for you?

6. Are there some areas where you need to learn how to say no so you can be faithful in the more important areas of life? Where do you need to say no? Is saying no hard for you? Why?

Faithfulness is such a rare commodity in our culture. Your faithfulness is sure to have an effect for good on those around you.

10

Step Eight
Gentleness

Let your gentleness be evident to all. The Lord is near.
Philippians 4:5

When I was a teenager I got a job picking asparagus for
Walter Lotts, a dear friend of the family and an elder in our
church. It was the first job I ever had, walking up and down
the rows of his farm, cutting asparagus with a special tool.

I was quite impressed with Walter Lotts, and one of the reasons for that was that he drove a Cadillac. He was the first
person I ever knew who drove such a fancy car.

One day he sent me to get something out of the trunk of
that Cadillac, which I did. But when I went to close the trunk,
I couldn't get it to shut. I slammed it down, but it bounced
back up. So I slammed it again, harder this time. Once again
it bounced back open. Several times I tried to get that trunk
to shut and several times I failed.

My boss was watching all this, with a somewhat bemused
look on his face. After several more of my futile attempts, he

strolled leisurely over to me, shaking his head, and took me by the hand.

"Always treat things like you treat a baby," he said. Then slowly, gently, without forcing it at all, he pulled that trunk lid down and it automatically locked into place as pretty as you please.

Of course I was embarrassed but I also knew that I'd learned an important lesson. It has stayed with me since then. "Always treat things like you treat a baby." There is some very good advice in those words.

I was only four years old when my sister Jeannie was born. I can still remember how excited and grown-up I felt to hold my little sister in my arms. Perhaps you, too, can remember the first time you held a baby—the gentle, soft way you held the baby, afraid that you might do something wrong that would cause him or her to break.

That's the way we need to learn to treat people's feelings.

We could all use a whole lot more of godly gentleness— the balanced blend of stability plus consideration, tact, understanding, and compassion.

Ask people what traits they admire most in others, and gentleness is not likely to rank high on the list. Why not? Because gentleness is just so . . . well . . . gentle. It doesn't draw attention to itself. And yet gentleness is such an important part of a good character that we all want our sons to behave "like gentlemen."

The person who is truly gentle is often relegated to the background. He or she is the one who is spending time meeting the needs of others, listening while the other person talks, as willing to learn as to teach.

The gentle person is rarely in the limelight, but he is often the one about whom others say, "I like that guy . . . there's just something about him." There is an attractive quality about a gentle spirit that others can't help but admire and like.

Gentleness is also the eighth fruit of the Spirit listed in Galatians 5:22. It is the eighth of the nine important ingredients that work together in a healthy, godly, workable personal system of morality.

The Greek word that is translated in Galatians as *gentleness* is *prautes*, which is a word the Greeks used to refer to people or things that had a soothing quality. For instance a lotion or ointment that used to take the sting out of a burn or insect bite would have been described as *prautes*. The word was also used to describe the atmosphere that ought to be maintained in a classroom setting, where people should feel free to discuss various ideas and beliefs without becoming overly defensive or argumentative.

Prautes was used to describe someone who had the ability to wield the power of the sword but who refused to behave as a tyrant. A king who chose to be merciful to his subjects would have been described in this way. Plato called *prautes* "the cement of society," and it's easy to see that such a gentle attitude would contribute toward peace and harmony.

What the Bible Has to Say about Gentleness

It is obvious to any Bible scholar that gentleness is a quality that is pleasing to God.

Philippians 4:5 tells us, "Let your gentleness be evident to all." Colossians 3:12 adds to this: "Therefore, as God's chosen people, holy and dearly loved, clothe yourselves with compassion, kindness, humility, gentleness and patience." The Bible also tells us that gentleness is something to be pursued:

"But you, man of God . . . pursue righteousness, godliness, faith, love, endurance and gentleness" (1 Tim. 6:11).

Billy Graham writes:

> An illustration that has helped me to understand gentleness is the iceberg. I have seen some of them from shipboard when crossing the Atlantic. However high an iceberg may be above the water line, the greater part of it is submerged. Icebergs are particularly formidable and destructive when they drift along the sea lanes.
>
> But the greatest threat to icebergs comes from something beneficent, the sun. The sun's rays bring warmth to life, and death to icebergs. As gentleness is a powerful force, so the sun proves to be more powerful than the mightiest iceberg. God's gentleness, or meekness, in us permits the rays of the sun of God's Holy Spirit to work on our icebound hearts, transforming them into instruments for good and for God. Spiritually, the gentle, Spirit-filled Christian is a prism through whom the rays of the sun's spectrum are gathered to minister to the icebergs of our carnality.[1]

Modern society seems to believe that greatness comes from a combination of opportunity, talent, and aggressiveness. But a theme that runs throughout the Bible is that true greatness comes from living according to God's laws and standards and recognizing that all we have does not come from our own ability and effort but from the gentleness of God's grace and mercy.

The apostle Peter says in 1 Peter 3:15–16:

> Always be prepared to give an answer to everyone who asks you to give the reason for the hope that you have. But do this with gentleness and respect, keeping a clear conscience, so that those who speak maliciously against your good behavior in Christ may be ashamed of their slander.

To get a proper understanding of this verse, you have to understand something of the persecution being faced by Christians in Peter's day.

Because Christians were different and because they refused to acknowledge the gods of the state, people were suspicious of them. Because Christians spoke of eating the flesh and drinking the blood of Christ, they were suspected of cannibalism. It was said that when they came together, they engaged in all sorts of bizarre rituals.

Believing such lies made it easier to persecute Christians, who were viewed as treasonous and evil. Christians were thrown into prison on false charges. Many were torn apart by lions. Thousands of them followed their Lord in crucifixion. It is reported that the emperor Nero sometimes lit up his gardens for parties at night by crucifying Christians and then setting them on fire.

When Peter wrote the books of the Bible that bear his name, this persecution of Christians had not yet reached its height, but persecution was taking place. It would not have been easy for anyone to maintain a gentle attitude in the face of it. Yet that's precisely what Peter urges his readers to do, to maintain a spirit of gentleness even when being questioned and criticized by people who not only didn't believe the way they did, but also didn't think they had a right to believe as they did and who may have been plotting against them because of their faith.

Gentleness is a recurring theme in Peter's writings, in marked contrast to his brash, rough and tough character, evident in the Gospels. (For example, see Mark 8:31–33 and John 13:6–9.) Over the years as he walked with God, the Holy Spirit changed Peter's personality, molding it to God's use and imparting to him a spirit of gentleness.

In the same way God is ready and willing to produce gentleness in your life and in mine.

Handle with Care

Have you ever heard it said that someone or other "values things and uses people"? Obviously that's not a very complimentary description.

The gentle person is just the opposite. That person values people and uses things. In other words, he or she understands that people have innate worth simply because they are human beings. He or she understands that people are not "things"; they are living, breathing spirits, created in the image of God, and that gives them inestimable worth.

Think about the intricacy and uniqueness of each human being:

- Nobody else, out of the five billion other people in the world, has the same fingerprints you have.
- The experiences you have had in life are unique to you. No one else understands and knows exactly what you understand and know.
- If all of the blood vessels in the human body were stretched out end to end, they would reach for more than 180,000 miles—or all the way around the earth more than seven times!
- Try as hard as they might, scientists have never come close to duplicating the efficiency and flexibility of the human brain.

The gentle person understands the uniqueness of the human individual and so is careful in relationships. You might say the gentle person treats other people as if they were wearing "handle with care" tags—as if they were fragile.

You know what? Human beings *are* fragile. They *do* need to be handled with care.

A gentle person is someone who understands that even when it's necessary to "get on somebody's case" about something, he or she doesn't have to be rude. The gentle person knows that it is possible to be firm and yet gentle at the same time.

In the book *Breaking Down Walls* Raleigh Washington, who is African American, writes about such an experience with a white employer:

When I was a young teenager, I worked three or four summers for a kindly but firm white grocer named Albert Soud. He taught me how to cut meat, weigh it, and package it, and allowed me to be his unofficial butcher.

One day a girl who lived with her single mom and four other kids in the apartment above us came into the store and asked for twenty-five cents worth of baloney. The family was very poor, so I sliced about three times that much, wrapped it up, and wrote twenty-five cents on the package. When the girl took it to the counter at the front to pay for it, Mr. Soud looked at the package and threw it on his own scale beside the cash register. Then he rolled his eyes at me, paused, and finally said to the girl, "Twenty-five cents, please."

Mr. Soud knew what I had done. Oh man, I'm going to get fired now, I thought. About thirty minutes later the shop closed, and I was busy cleaning up—doing a double good job—when Mr. Soud said, "Sit down, Raleigh, I want to tell you something. What you did was wrong. I work hard to try to make ends meet, and you defrauded me. I believe you were trying to help that young lady, but you helped her at my expense. The next time you want to help somebody and you think the reason is valid, ask me, and I will respond to you. But don't steal from me."

I was hurt and humbled; it was a lesson I never forgot. Even though I had wronged him, he was sensitive to the reason for my action. And he had been sensitive at the cash register, not willing to embarrass me in front of the girl.

Even though I had wronged him, Albert Soud had talked to me with respect, like a father would talk to his son. Even though I hated injustice and didn't like what was happening to my people, I developed a real love for that man.[2]

How many teenagers, do you suppose, are afraid to admit their mistakes to their parents because they know what's going to happen? Dad's going to "blow a gasket," or whatever the current terminology might be, and Mom's going to "have a cow." In other words, the response is not going to be gentle. I am convinced that if more parents would learn to be gentle but firm, we would see a vast improvement in parent-child relationships in this country.

It's only by the grace of God that any of us can maintain an attitude of gentleness, especially in the face of the pressures and problems of our fast-paced world. Most of us run into plenty of reasons to lose our temper just about every day, and it's easier to tell somebody off than to react with gentleness and understanding.

If you want to know how far you have to go in the area of gentleness, let me make a suggestion: Come and spend a week driving on the freeways of Southern California. You'll find out very quickly how close you are to having a gentle spirit.

I'm being facetious, of course, but my point is that gentleness needs to be cultivated, that it is developed over time as you walk with God.

In her book *The Spirituality of Gentleness* Judith C. Lechman writes that some twenty-three times in both the Old and New Testaments the Bible calls to gentleness those who believe in God:

> From the Psalms and Zechariah to Matthew and Peter, gentleness is demanded of us in our conduct with God and one another. In each scriptural reference to gentleness, we are given a distinct invitation to imitate Christ and model ourselves after him.
>
> God initiates gentleness. We respond. Christ calls us to gentleness. We answer. When he commands us to follow him, to accept his plans for us, to commit ourselves wholeheartedly to him, and

to go the way he goes without questioning, we struggle to echo his gentleness in our attitude and behavior.[3]

Cultivating Gentleness

In my own life, even though I learned an important lesson on the subject from Walter Lotts and his Cadillac, treating others gently did not come naturally or easily for me. Over the years I've often been accused of being rather abrupt and to-the-point, of lacking in gentleness.

Then I spent a week studying with Dr. David Burns, the father of cognitive therapy, who is widely regarded as one of the foremost thinkers in America today. I learned a great deal from Dr. Burns, primarily about "responsive listening."

Responsive listening is simply repeating what you think you heard the other person say. That way you know for sure that you are understanding the person properly.

Have you ever had a conversation with someone in which something was said that hit you the wrong way? Perhaps you didn't think much about it at first, but later that day—probably at night when you were trying to drift off to sleep—it came back to you and you started thinking, *I wonder what he meant by that.* Or, *Hey! I think she was insulting me.*

If so, what happened next? Probably this: The more you thought about it, the more you were sure something had been said that was meant to hurt you, and pretty soon you're really angry at the other person.

Responsive listening doesn't allow that to happen. It involves rephrasing the other person's statement in such a way that he or she can say, "Yes, that's exactly what I meant" or else, "No, you've misunderstood me. Let me explain."

I'm convinced that many arguments are the result of mis-communication—reading something into what somebody said that they really didn't mean. I am convinced that if respon-sive listening were practiced in every household throughout America, the divorce rate would drop considerably.

In *The Feeling Good Handbook* Dr. Burns lists five secrets of effective communication.[4] I believe that these five skills, all of which are related to responsive listening, can contribute greatly to the cause of gentleness.

1. The disarming technique. This means finding some truth in what the other person is saying, even if you really think that the comment being made is "totally wrong, unreasonable, irrational, or unfair."
2. Empathy. You put yourself in the other person's place and attempt to see the situation the way he or she does. In "thought empathy" you paraphrase what other people say to make sure you have heard them right, and in "feel-ing empathy" you "acknowledge how they're probably feeling, given what they are saying to you."
3. Inquiry. This involves asking "gentle, probing questions" so that you can come to a better understanding of what the other person is thinking and feeling.
4. "I feel" statements. This involves making statements that begin with "I feel" rather than "You are." When you make "I feel" statements, you are explaining how you are interpreting what is being said, but you are not accus-ing the other person and putting him or her on the defensive. Saying, "I feel upset by what you're saying" is much gentler and more conducive to continued con-versation than saying, "You're wrong about that" or, "You're being unfair!"

5. Stroking. In stroking you find something positive to say to the other person, even if you are in the middle of a heated argument. This shows the other person that you respect him or her, even though you may be angry with each other at the moment.

Dr. Burns goes on to explain the art of responsive listening:

Once you have paraphrased what the other person said, acknowledge the feelings he or she might have and ask a question to see if you are reading his or her emotions correctly. Suppose your husband suddenly jumps on you by saying: "Why don't you ever listen? Trying to talk to you is like beating my head against a brick wall!" Using feeling empathy, you could respond: "It sounds like I've been closed-minded and stubborn. I can imagine that you might be feeling fed up and frustrated with me. Do you feel that way?" As he begins to ventilate about how he feels, accept his feelings instead of reacting in a critical or hostile way (the aggressive response) or withdrawing and playing the role of wounded victim (the passive response). If he says, "Damn right I'm upset!" you can then say, "I'm glad you told me that, even though this is upsetting to me. I get pretty frustrated when people don't listen to me, so I can understand how you're feeling." This response involves resisting your all-too-human urge to lash out and fight back. You'll probably be feeling just as hurt and angry as he is, and you'll understandably want to prove that he's wrong. Don't.[5]

Responsive listening produces gentleness in two ways. First, it improves communication and understanding between human beings, and any time that happens mistrust and disharmony are less likely; and second, it lets the other person know that what he or she is saying is important enough to me that I want to make sure I heard it right.

Responsive listening may sound easy but it really isn't. It takes lots and lots of practice to get it right, but it is worth the effort it takes.

I practice it with my children. For example, one morning recently I told Anthony I wanted him to do three things before he left for school: make his bed, brush his teeth, and comb his hair.

"You got it?" I asked him.

"You bet, Dad."

"Okay, Anthony. Now what is it I want you to do?"

"Ummmmm . . ." His little brow wrinkled and he squinted his eyes, as if he were deep in thought.

"Okay, Anthony, I want you to listen to me this time. I want you to go upstairs and make your bed. Then I want you to brush your teeth and comb your hair."

"Okay."

"Now tell me what it is I want you to do."

"Make my bed and . . ." That blank, thoughtful look was back.

"Give me your hand, Anthony." He held out his hand, and I took it into mine. "There are three things I want you to do."

I pointed to his index finger.

"One, I want you to make your bed."

Then I pointed to his middle finger.

"Two, I want you to brush your teeth . . . and three," we pointed together at the next finger, "I want you to comb your hair."

"Okay, I got it."

And he did. When I asked him again to tell me what it was that I wanted him to do, he dutifully pointed at the three fingers and repeated everything I had told him. Then he marched upstairs and . . . made his bed, brushed his teeth, and combed his hair.

There was a time not too long ago when I would have told Anthony what I wanted him to do and he would have said,

"You bet, Dad" and gone merrily about his business. He might have made his bed, although I'm not too sure about that. He most certainly wouldn't have given his teeth a second thought, and he would have run out of the house with his hair looking as if he were trying out for the part of Albert Einstein in a school play.

But because we practice responsive listening, I can count on Anthony to do what I want him to do—most of the time anyway—and that results in much more peace and gentleness in the Schuller household.

Do You Know What Your Gifts Are?

At Rancho Capistrano Community Church we practice responsive listening, and we also strive to develop a spirit of gentleness through gaining an understanding of how God has gifted us as individual members of the church. We then strive to establish and maintain boundaries according to our individual gifts.

In the last chapter we talked about the importance of establishing personal boundaries in the area of faithfulness because it's impossible to be faithful to everyone who wants your time and attention. Such boundaries are also important to the development of gentleness.

In this instance, the boundaries should be established through the process of coming to recognize what your spiritual gifts are and what God expects you to do with those gifts. I believe that God has gifted every believer with specific talents and abilities. I also believe he calls each believer to use those talents and abilities in specific ways.

Understanding God's calling on your life can keep you from getting pushed and pulled in a number of different directions at once. When you are using your talents and abilities as God wants you to use them, you will have a feeling of contentment and satisfaction. You will not feel harried and angry and you will begin to develop a gentle spirit.

It's not my purpose here to tell you how to discover your gifts, but I will say that it is important to pray about it. It's also important to seek the advice of those whose wisdom and spiritual maturity you trust. There are a number of excellent surveys and tests you can take to help you discern what your specific gifts might be. If you don't know what your gifts are or don't have any idea what God has called you to do, do yourself a favor and take steps to find out.

Then if someone asks you to do something that's outside the calling God has placed on your life, you can gently say no, you can't do that, simply because it is not something for which you are gifted. You don't have to be rude. You don't have to lie and make up an excuse. You can be gentle but firm in your refusal.

It seems to me that most people don't know how to say no politely and gently. Instead, they say things like, "I don't have time." To me, that's about the worst reason you can give someone, because the implication is "I don't have time for you. I'm too busy to be bothered by whatever it is you want me to do."

When you know what your priorities are and have an understanding of how God has gifted you, then you can simply say, "I'm really not gifted in this area. I know there's someone else who can do a much better job than I could ever do." After that, you need to share your gifts with others. Let other people know where you are going and what God is doing in your life and invite them to be a part of your journey.

Gentleness doesn't exclude people. It enfolds them. It reaches out to them with love. That may sound like a con-

tradiction, since we've been talking about drawing boundaries, but those boundaries are not there to keep other people
out of your life. Instead, they can serve to keep your relationships healthy, enabling you to relate to others based on
a proper self-image of who you are in God and a right understanding of the gifts and priorities he has given you.

A Closer Look at Gentleness

Judith C. Lechman says this about gentleness:

To put the biblical command to be gentle into action in our lives
we need the power of the Spirit. With it, we can live a life free of
the fear of persecution, suffering, and punishment; we know the
end of bitterness and resentment, too. The power that comes from
the Spirit enables us to grow in courage, wisdom, and responsibility to and for others.[6]

She goes on to say:

Through the Spirit, our soul begins to see what is meant by gentleness. Clinging to this vision, we enact it in our lives and find,
to our surprise, that we already see more clearly how better we
may live gentleness. Action, vision, and deeper insight escalate
and fuse, so that we recognize both the widening scope of gentleness needed in our lives and the conditions demanded to
accomplish it.
    Empowered by the Spirit, the quality of our actions bears direct
witness to the gentleness of God. What we tell others about God's
gentleness in our lives is less convincing than how we live that gentleness. Truly gentle Christians, who are filled with the power of
the Spirit, will become worthy signposts, pointing to divine gentleness by the way they treat those in the world around them.
Although teaching, preaching, and writing are valid ways of proclaiming God's gentleness, the most effective sermon is the man-
ner in which we act to radiate the divine sparks.[7]

Are You Gentle?

Answer these questions to help discover where in your life you need to be more gentle.

1. Proverbs 15:1 tells us that "a gentle answer turns away wrath, but a harsh word stirs up anger." Can you think of some personal experiences where the truth of this proverb has been borne out?
2. First Peter 3:9 says, "Do not repay evil with evil or insult with insult, but with blessing." How difficult is it for you to do this? If it is hard for you, why do you think this is the case?
3. What do you think would happen in our society if we all tried to live in obedience to the words of the apostle Peter quoted above?
4. Can you think of any incidents recently in which another person displayed gentleness toward you? How did that experience make you feel?
5. I told you about two people in my life who have helped me learn what it means to be gentle: Walter Lotts and Dr. David Burns. Are there some people in your life who have taught you similar lessons? If so, who are they, and how did they teach you about gentleness?
6. Can you think of some particular situations in which it would be hard for you not to react angrily or defensively? How do you think you can change your attitude so you can demonstrate a gentler spirit in such circumstances?

11

Step Nine
Self-Control

He is most powerful who has power over himself.
Seneca

In this chapter we come to the last of our moral building blocks, self-control, something about which the Bible says: "Better a patient man than a warrior, a man who controls his temper than one who takes a city" (Prov. 16:32).

Really, self-control is God-control. Only the person who is yielded to God's Spirit will be able to develop this attribute. Christianity contains many paradoxes. For example, Jesus said, "Whoever finds his life will lose it, and whoever loses his life for my sake will find it" (Matt. 10:39).

Similarly, the man or woman who seeks to maintain control over his or her life will most likely find that things are out of control, but the person who gives up control of his or her life to God will find that he or she has the ability to control himself or herself.

The Importance of Self-Control

Take a look at the crime rate, the spread of AIDS, and all the problems of modern society, and that's just the beginning of what things would be like if we all abandoned the concept of self-control and lived according to one of the rallying cries of the sixties: "If it feels good, do it." If we all did whatever we wanted, whenever we wanted, our society would be much worse than it is.

Self-control is vitally important, in all areas of life. Billy Graham says:

> The need for temperance [self-control] in every aspect of life has never been greater than it is today. At a time when violence, self-ishness, apathy, and undisciplined living threaten to destroy this planet, it is imperative that Christians set an example. The world needs this example—something steadfast it can hold on to, an anchor in a raging sea.

He adds that some people

> have an elastic conscience when it comes to their own foibles—and an ironbound conscience when it comes to the foibles of others. Maybe that's why it is so easy for some Christians to condemn a person who takes an occasional sip of wine but never rebuke themselves for the sin of habitual overeating. Compulsive overeating is one of the most widely accepted and practiced sins of modern Western Christians. It is easy to condemn an adulterer, but how can the one who condemns do so when he is guilty of some other form of intemperance? Should each one of us not have clean hands and a pure heart in all of life? Is one form of slavery more wrong in principle than another? Are we not just as tightly bound if the chains are made of ropes as of steel?[1]

The importance of self-control is a theme that runs throughout the Bible's pages. Here are just some of the areas where God tells us that self-control is required.

- When we are angry. Proverbs 14:29 says, "A patient man has great understanding, but a quick-tempered man displays folly."
- When we are tempted to give in to improper desires. Second Timothy 2:22 says, "Flee the evil desires of youth, and pursue righteousness, faith, love and peace, along with those who call on the Lord out of a pure heart."
- When we are tempted to talk too much. Ephesians 4:29 says, "Do not let any unwholesome talk come out of your mouths, but only what is helpful for building others up according to their needs, that it may benefit those who listen."
- When it comes to eating. First Corinthians 10:31–32 says, "So whether you eat or drink or whatever you do, do it all for the glory of God. Do not cause anyone to stumble, whether Jews, Greeks or the church of God."
- When it comes to money. As Matthew 6:19–21 says, "Do not store up for yourselves treasures on earth, where moth and rust destroy, and where thieves break in and steal. But store up for yourselves treasures in heaven, where moth and rust do not destroy, and where thieves do not break in and steal. For where your treasure is, there your heart will be also."

According to the apostle Peter, self-control is an important step in building a life that is pleasing to God. In 2 Peter 1:2–10 he writes:

Everything that goes into a life of pleasing God has been miraculously given to us by getting to know, personally and intimately, the One who invited us to God. The best invitation we ever received! We were also given absolutely terrific promises to pass on

to you—your tickets to participation in the life of God after you
turned your back on a world corrupted by lust.

So don't lose a minute in building on what you've been given,
complementing your basic faith with good character, spiritual
understanding, alert discipline, passionate patience, reverent wonder, warm friendliness, and generous love, each dimension fitting
into and developing the others. With these qualities active and
growing in your lives, no grass will grow under your feet, no day
will pass without its reward as you mature in your experience of our
Master Jesus. Without these qualities you can't see what's right
before you, oblivious that your old sinful life has been wiped off the
books.

THE MESSAGE

God expects all of his people to develop the qualities Peter
writes about. They will come to us as we grow closer to God
every step of the way through life, counting on God to give
us his own character, including self-control.

Getting closer to God takes patience and persistence.
Some people are tempted to give up after a few halfhearted
attempts. Learning to know God better and better takes faith,
focus, and follow-through, so don't give up. When you get
to know him better as a loving Father, you will also learn to
seek and ask for what is good for you, including the virtue of
self-control.

The Great Debate

When we look seriously at the topic of self-control, we find
ourselves embroiled in a theological debate that has been
raging for centuries. It is the classic debate between the concept of the free will of mankind and the sovereignty of God.
I believe that theologians will be arguing about those two
aspects of man's relationship to God until the world ends.

The debate starts with an examination of the sovereignty of God. We all know that God is sovereign, which means that he is all-powerful, all-knowing, all-everything. Nothing can take place without his knowledge or permission.

Well, if that's the case, the question goes, then what role do we human beings play in life? Do we have freedom to do anything without God's intervention? Can we tie our shoes without his involvement? Can we brush our teeth? Do we really have the freedom to do anything, or is it all planned out for us?

In other words, at what point do we take responsibility for our actions, and at what point is God responsible? Some people go so far as to say, "It doesn't matter what I do, because God is responsible anyway. He made me the way I am and there's nothing I can do about it."

I've even talked to people who were angry with God about the way they've messed up their lives: "He knew when he made me that this was going to happen to me. I don't think he's very fair."

How do you respond to people who feel that way?

Prayer and Work Go Hand in Hand

More than fifteen hundred years ago Augustine made a statement that, to me, neatly ties up the debate regarding how we are to live and work and understand our relationship with God.

Augustine said that we should pray as if everything depended on God but then work as if it all depended on us. This is a wonderful statement that clarifies the balance between the sovereignty of God and the free will of man.

I want to talk to you specifically about three important areas where we need to do as Augustine said, praying as if everything depended on God and working as if it all depended on us: emotions, outcomes, and destiny.

Emotions

It is important to always remember that you cannot control your emotions, but you can control your actions. You cannot control how you feel when things happen to you. If something happens to you that makes you feel sad, you can't change it just by saying, "I don't want to feel sad anymore." On the other hand, you don't have to express your sadness to others.

If you're driving on the freeway and some nut cuts you off, you're probably going to feel angry, but you don't have to vent your anger. You don't have to pull up alongside him and shake your fist at him or swear at him or—as some have done in California in recent years—shoot him. You can find a better, more constructive way to release your anger. When you do that, you are exhibiting godly self-control.

There is an old Chinese fable about a man who decides that he wants to become a monk and so goes to the monastery for studies. The first day when he meets his teacher, the teacher pulls out a stick and says, "This stick is not a stick. Tell me what it is or I'll hit you with it."

The man doesn't know what to do. It sure looks like a stick to him. But finally he says, "It is a twig."

The teacher hits him with the stick and says, "Your lesson today is over. You may leave."

The next day the man comes back to talk to the teacher again. He is dismayed to see that the teacher is carrying the same stick and even more dismayed when he says the same thing he said the day before: "This stick is not a stick. Tell me what it is or I'll hit you with it."

"Umm . . . uh . . ." finally the fellow has another idea. "It's a branch."

Wrong answer.

Once again the teacher hits him with the stick, tells him that the day's lesson is over, and sends him on his way.

For days the same thing continues. The man makes all sorts of guesses regarding what this "stick" really might be. Is it a whip? A club? A cane? Every day the teacher rejects his answer and hits him again.

Finally, he's had enough. So when the teacher pulls out the stick and says, "Tell me what it is or I'm going to hit you with it," the man says, "Oh, no you're not." He grabs the stick out of his teacher's hands, breaks it over his knee, and throws it out the window.

The teacher smiles at him, "Well done. You have learned your lesson well."

The teacher was not interested in getting his pupil to describe the stick. Instead, he was interested in teaching him that he had the ability to make an important choice—a choice that could keep him from being hurt. We all have the ability to make the same sort of choices.

The monk in that story had three options. He could try to find the right answer so he wouldn't be hit. He could just sit there and take it. Or he could grab the stick and throw it out the window.

Not until he exercised the right option, did he find relief. Only then did he show that he had learned the importance of self-control.

When bad things happen to you, you can analyze why you feel the way you do: *Why am I so angry? Why did this make me so afraid? Why do I feel so sad?* But you don't have to let your emotions beat you up. You don't have to let them get you to respond in ways that are destructive to you or to other people in your life.

Self-control means getting to the place where you have control over your emotions—where they do not have control over you.

Outcomes

You cannot control the outcome of a situation but you can control your next step.

We all make plans for our life. We set goals and make decisions designed to fulfill those goals. We all have hopes and dreams. We don't always get what we want as we pursue those goals. The outcome is not always favorable. In spite of that, we should all understand that God has designed our outcomes for us.

Let me give you an example from my personal experience. I was passing through a very emotional time in my life. In one week I rode the roller coaster from the top of the mountain all the way down into the deepest valley.

The week began on a very positive note when I got the chance to fish with some friends in a prestigious deep-sea tournament. We took third place and I was thrilled. It was just a tremendous, fun time with my friends.

Then the next morning I received an extremely disappointing fax. The fax had to do with a decision our church made to start a school, Rancho Capistrano School, for students in first through sixth grades. Our initial plan was to have our first classes underway by September of that year.

Once we had made the decision to open the school, the first thing we did was hire teachers, who then put in their resignations at their current jobs so they would be ready to work for us. Then we began taking applications and deposits from students who wanted to enroll in our school. At the same time, those students had to send notices to their current schools saying they would not be coming back. In addition to that, we started negotiating with various contractors to build the classrooms we needed. We had all of the plans designed and everything was ready to go.

Then we got news from the county that we couldn't have a school on our property until we received a school-use permit and we couldn't get one without several public hearings, and so forth. When I asked how quickly all of this could be accomplished, I was told that it could be done in two or three months.

Two or three months? It was June already. We needed to be ready to open our doors for classes around the first of September. If it was going to take two or three months, then I couldn't get building permits until August at the earliest. Once I had those permits, there would still be two or three months of construction facing us—at the very least. It all seemed so impossible.

I sat down to make a list of possible options, even though at first glance there didn't seem to be any. But I've been around long enough to know that you're never out of options with God.

I went down to the county courthouse to see if anyone there could help me and I was eventually directed to a wonderful man who told me what to do. He said we could get a permit to build classrooms for our Sunday school classes. Then once we got the school-use permit we could use those classrooms for the school.

"You just have to promise me," he said, "that you won't use those classrooms for a school until you have a school permit." He asked me to write him a letter to that affect, which I was happy to do.

We went through all sorts of difficult negotiations and maneuvers to get our school built and ready on time. By the day of the fishing tournament, I thought everything had been worked out to everyone's satisfaction.

Wrong!

Wednesday morning I came home from the tournament higher than a kite only to find that unsettling fax, which came from the city of San Juan Capistrano. Seems I'd been so busy jumping through all of the county's hoops that I hadn't figured on the city fathers having a few hoops of their own.

The city was insisting that the school project be postponed indefinitely until a number of conditions were met—and it would take several years to meet those conditions. They wanted a master plan for the land that included major improvements like roads, flood control channels, and all sorts of things that were totally out of our control.

Once again it seemed that I had run up against a brick wall. What did I do?

I sat down and decided what my options were. Then I started calling everyone I could think of who worked for the city or county and told them that I had to meet with them right away. The next few days blurred together into a series of meetings, challenges, and counter-challenges. Through it all, God was faithful. The final result was that our use permit was finally granted a little later than scheduled, but our school was able to open its doors in an acceptable time frame.

I was never able, at any point, to control what the outcome of my negotiations might be, either with the county or with the city, but I was always able to control my next step. With God's help and guidance, things worked out very well.

It certainly wasn't easy. There were a number of times when I felt like giving up. But even when it looked hopeless, there were always other options available to me.

Allow me to use another example from my personal experience. I started out in college as a music major. In my junior year there were two required classes that I needed to take. One was a prerequisite for the other. I obtained special permission to take both of them at the same time because they were only offered once every two years. If I didn't take them then I would have to return to college for a fifth year. When I went to register I discovered that they were scheduled at exactly the same time. There was no way I could take both of them that year. I had two choices. I could stay in college longer than planned or I could change my major.

I looked at the options and decided to change my major from music to ancient civilization, which was really the only other choice I had. It turned out to be the best thing I could have done. Ancient civilization was terrific preparation for going into the ministry, which was what I really wanted to do all along.

My point is that you always have options, which God will use to lead you to his desired outcome. Even when you feel like your back is against the wall and you're about to give up, God can help you find a way out.

Destiny

What is your destiny? It's the point in life at which you look around you and realize that you are in the right place and you are happy with your life. That's when you've determined your personal destiny. Because that's true, it is important that you take steps in the direction you really want to travel. If you live in Chicago and want to go to New York, don't go west and blame God when you find yourself in Los Angeles. How sad it is to wake up one morning and decide that you hate where you are in life.

Still, you can't always control your destiny. You don't always end up where you wanted to be when you began your journey no matter how proactive you are.

My destiny is in the ministry at Rancho Capistrano Community Church and the Crystal Cathedral Ministries. I didn't plan it. It just happened. I looked at my options, took the best one, and moved forward. Over time, my destiny developed to a point where it is today. I never consider doing anything else because I love what I'm doing and I am very happy with my ministry.

I spent twenty years in school studying for the ministry. But if I were unhappy and unfulfilled, I would go back to school or start doing what I felt would be more rewarding, even if I were sixty-five or seventy years old. You are rarely too old to create your destiny. In Genesis 6:3 God says of man, "he is mortal; his days will be a hundred and twenty years." In Deuteronomy we have the record of Moses' death. It says he was one hundred and twenty years old and was healthy until the day he died. I believe these words and am planning my life accordingly. Let's be conservative and say you'll only live to be one hundred. If that's true, how many years do you have left to fulfill your calling and follow your destiny?

Consider Colonel Sanders, the founder of Kentucky Fried Chicken. He was sixty-five years old when he lost everything he owned. He had a tiny chicken shack on the side of the road. Then a major highway came through the area and completely bypassed his little restaurant. Nobody stopped anymore.

Sanders was down the tubes with nothing but a recipe for fried chicken. Faced with his options he went out, at the age of sixty-five, and created what we know today as Kentucky Fried Chicken. He did it because he had lost everything. If the highway hadn't changed, we never would have heard of KFC!

He didn't plan to found a billion-dollar restaurant chain, but when he was stripped of what little he had accumulated over the years, he considered his options, decided that he did have something of value, and used that to take his next step forward in life.

You see, you don't decide your destiny. Things happen. Outcomes are created. All you decide is your next step along the path, and then God uses that to craft the destiny he has in mind for you. When we live in the Spirit, God directs our steps in ways we cannot imagine, he closes doors we do not expect, and he turns evil into good for those who believe.

Self-Control and God's Plan

What does all this have to do with self-control? In many of the situations life brings your way, you have to exercise self-control to make the decisions that will be appropriate and right. You are faced with options all along the way and you have to choose the right one—the step that will lead you closer to God and to fulfillment of his purpose for your life.

It is only in fulfilling God's purpose for you that you will be at peace—contented and at rest in a world full of disappointment and turbulence. In Matthew 7:7–12 Jesus says:

Ask and it will be given to you; seek and you will find; knock and the door will be opened to you. For everyone who asks receives; he who seeks finds; and to him who knocks, the door will be opened.

Which of you, if his son asks for bread, will give him a stone? Or if he asks for a fish, will give him a snake? If you, then, though you are evil, know how to give good gifts to your children, how much more will your Father in heaven give good gifts to those who ask him! So in everything, do to others what you would have them do to you, for this sums up the Law and the Prophets.

God knows the destiny that's best for you. He knows what you need, even before you know! He also knows that there are times when we think we're asking him for something beneficial, but the truth is that we're asking for something that might really hurt us—that might move us in the wrong direction in life.

We may not be aware of it, but he is, and that's why there are times when he has to say no. But whether he says yes or no, you can rest in the knowledge that he has acted in your best interests, that his actions in your behalf are borne out of his loving Father's heart.

How Are You at Controlling Yourself?

How do you measure up in the area of self-control? Let's take a closer look:

1. The dictionary defines self-control as "restraint exercised over one's own impulses, emotions, or desires." Keeping this definition in mind, would you say that you are a self-controlled person? In what areas of your life do you feel you exercise the most self-control? The least? What would you like to change about your ability to exercise self-control?

2. Can you think of a time when a lack of self-control caused harm to you or someone else? What happened and why? What should have been done differently?

3. Verses 18 through 32 of Romans 1 give us a picture of life in a world without personal self-control. After read-

ing this passage, can you come up with a list of benefits to society that result from the exercise of self-control?

4. Self-control is a virtue that can be attained only through the power of God's Spirit. Keeping that in mind, ask yourself if your current relationship with God is as personal and intimate as it might be. Do you see any correlation between your level of intimacy with God and the presence or lack of self-control in your life?

5. In Matthew 7:7–12 Jesus paints a picture of God as an all-knowing and benevolent Father who always gives his children what is best for them. In what ways have you personally experienced this nature of God? How does seeing God in this way affect the level of self-control you are able to exercise in your life?

PART 3

Putting It All Together

12

Lessons from the Life of Christ

I have set you an example.
Jesus Christ (John 13:15)

We have been talking about the search for morality—more specifically, about building a personal framework of morality that will hold up in these turbulent last days of the twentieth century.

We started out by seeing the error of thinking that morality has to do with obedience to the laws of the land. Even in a "Christian" nation such as the United States, there are laws that God-fearing people may consider to be immoral. On the other hand, there are many behaviors that God-fearing people would consider immoral that are not even mentioned in the laws of the land.

In many ways, our society seems to be completely out of control—without a moral anchor. Violence seems to be increasing. Many of our young people are evidently without conscience. We are bombarded through the media on a daily basis by messages that appeal to our basic instincts.

Where, in all of this mess, can you find a moral anchor for your life? To answer this question we have turned to the Bible, specifically to these words from the apostle Paul: "But the fruit of the Spirit is love, joy, peace, patience, kindness, goodness, faithfulness, gentleness and self-control" (Gal. 5:22).

We have looked at these nine fruit of the Spirit one at a time, seeing how the cultivation of each could change a person's life . . . indeed, could change the entire world. We've talked about how these nine fruit will help you build a life that is pleasing to God and therefore a life full of personal peace and contentment in a world that is often battered by war, confusion, and uncertainty.

We've seen how these various characteristics are interdependent; for example, how joy is dependent on love for God and love for self and how goodness sets limits on kindness. Now I want to spend these final few pages talking about the importance of putting all of these characteristics together.

When it comes to a life that demonstrates all of these fruit of the Spirit, there is one man who stands out above all other human beings.

That man is, of course, Jesus Christ.

The Bible tells us that in Christ the Holy Spirit was "without limit" (John 3:34). You would expect, then, to find in his life a perfect demonstration of the working of the fruit of the Spirit.

And you do. I want to take a brief look at his life, beginning with the first fruit, love.

Love

Jesus showed his love in many ways, as in this acount:

When he came down from the mountainside, large crowds followed him. A man with leprosy came and knelt before him and said, "Lord, if you are willing, you can make me clean."

Jesus reached out his hand and touched the man. "I am willing," he said. "Be clean!" Immediately he was cured of his leprosy.

Matthew 8:1–3

Two thousand years ago nobody wanted to get within shouting distance of a leper. Leprosy was believed to be extremely contagious, and victims of the disease were ostracized from the rest of society.

But in this instance Jesus reached out and touched the man, letting him know that he was loved and valued, providing the human contact he had been denied for so long. Through his loving touch I believe Jesus was healing the man emotionally as well as physically.

Of course Jesus' love for others is clearly seen in his sacrificial death on the cross but it can also be seen in the way he lived. He entered into situations where others would not go, taking the love of God to people whom others considered to be unlovely—lepers, the lame, the blind, prostitutes, tax collectors, and the like.

Wherever Jesus went, he built bridges between people and between people and God. Truly he showed us how to love by the way he fulfilled this verse from Isaiah:

> The Spirit of the Sovereign LORD is on me,
>   because the LORD has anointed me
>   to preach good news to the poor.
> He has sent me to bind up the brokenhearted,
>   to proclaim freedom for the captives
>   and release from darkness for the prisoners,
> to proclaim the year of the LORD's favor.
>
> *Isaiah 61:1–2*

Joy

Before he died Jesus said to his disciples:

> Now is your time of grief, but I will see you again and you will
> rejoice, and no one will take away your joy. In that day you will no
> longer ask me anything. I tell you the truth, my Father will give
> you whatever you ask in my name. Until now you have not asked
> for anything in my name. Ask and you will receive, and your joy
> will be complete.
>
> John 16:22–24

Somewhere along the line most people have picked up the
notion that Jesus went around with a sad, stern look on his
face, joyless, devoid of warmth and humor. It's simply not so.

It's true that Isaiah prophesied that he would be "a man of
sorrows" (Isa. 53:3), but he was also a man of great inner
strength and joy. Certainly he was on this earth to take care
of some very serious business but through it all he was joyful
because he knew he was carrying out his Father's will.

The Bible describes him as being "full of joy through the
Holy Spirit." In John 17:13, when Jesus prayed for his disciples, he said, "I say these things while I am still in the world,
so that they may have the full measure of my joy within them."

Regarding this passage of Scripture, Andrew Murray wrote:

> Christ's own joy, abiding joy, fullness of joy—such is the portion
> of the believer who abides in Christ. Why, O why is it that this
> joy has so little power to attract? The reason simply is: Men, yea,
> even God's children, do not believe in it. Instead of the abiding
> in Christ being looked upon as the happiest life that ever can be
> led, it is regarded as a life of self-denial and of sadness. They for-
> get that the self-denial and the sadness are owing to the not abid-
> ing, and that to those who once yield themselves unreservedly to
> abide in Christ as a bright and blessed life, their faith comes true—
> the joy of the Lord is theirs. The difficulties all arise from the want
> of the full surrender to a full abiding.[1]

Jesus often presented serious truths in a humorous, joyful way. For example, when he told his disciples that it would be easier for a camel to pass through the eye of a needle than for a rich man to enter heaven (Matt. 19:24), he was presenting a comical picture, and I'm sure that those who heard him laughed out loud at the idea.* The same was true when he talked of those who would "strain out a gnat but swallow a camel" (Matt. 23:24).

Peace

Jesus' peace was visible:

> That day when evening came, he said to his disciples, "Let us go over to the other side." Leaving the crowd behind, they took him along, just as he was, in the boat. There were also other boats with him. A furious squall came up, and the waves broke over the boat, so that it was nearly swamped. Jesus was in the stern, sleeping on a cushion. The disciples woke him and said to him, "Teacher, don't you care if we drown?"
>
> Mark 4:35–38

I love this story. There is Jesus, peacefully asleep while his disciples frantically try to keep their small boat from being swamped by the wind and the waves.

Jesus certainly knew that life has its stormy moments. Through it all he kept an eternal perspective. Even in the midst of a terrible storm he could sleep, knowing that he was safely and securely within the love of God.

---

*The eye of a needle is a small gate built into the larger city gate. This small gate was generally open while the huge city gates remained closed for security. Only one person at a time could pass through the eye of a needle, while an entire army could march through the city gate. It was difficult, of course, for a camel to pass through the eye of a needle and amusing to watch.

It is not easy to learn to rest while a storm is howling out-side your window. It comes through constant practice of giv-ing up your cares to God, of learning to follow the apostle Peter's admonition to "cast all your anxiety on him because he cares for you" (1 Peter 5:7).

Because Jesus knew how to do that, he could sleep in that little boat in the middle of a terrible storm. We would all save ourselves much grief if we could learn to live that way!

Patience

Think of the patience of Jesus.

At that time some Pharisees came to Jesus and said to him, "Leave this place and go somewhere else. Herod wants to kill you."

He replied, "Go tell that fox, 'I will drive out demons and heal people today and tomorrow, and on the third day I will reach my goal.' In any case, I must keep going today and tomorrow and the next day—for surely no prophet can die outside Jerusalem!

"O Jerusalem, Jerusalem, you who kill the prophets and stone those sent to you, how often I have longed to gather your children together, as a hen gathers her chicks under her wings, but you were not willing!"

Luke 13:31–34

Jesus continued to teach and heal and do good in the face of continuous opposition from the authorities. Everywhere he went, he did good for people, even though he knew that many of them would eventually turn against him, falsely ac-cuse him of crimes, and demand his execution.

Think of his patience as he walked with Judas Iscariot day after day, showing love and friendship for the man he knew would eventually betray him.

Think of his patience with the other disciples, who often misunderstood the nature of his mission here on earth. They looked for him to set up an earthly kingdom. In spite of his teachings on the importance of serving others, they fought over who would be greatest in that kingdom. They heard him talk about the importance of learning to love our enemies but still wanted to call down fire from heaven on the heads of those who opposed them. Then when Jesus needed them most, they deserted him.

One thing you can count on in this world is that people are going to let you down. That's a fact of life. That doesn't mean people are evil. It simply means they are weak; they don't always do what they mean to do or want to do.

That's just one of the reasons why patience is so very important. Without patience, you're going to have a very hard time in life. Remember, life's not a sprint; it's a marathon.

Kindness

The Pharisees loved to test Jesus.

The teachers of the law and the Pharisees brought in a woman caught in adultery. They made her stand before the group and said to Jesus, "Teacher, this woman was caught in the act of adultery. In the Law Moses commanded us to stone such women. Now what do you say?" They were using this question as a trap, in order to have a basis for accusing him.

But Jesus bent down and started to write on the ground with his finger. When they kept on questioning him, he straightened up and said to them, "If any one of you is without sin, let him be the first to throw a stone at her." Again he stooped down and wrote on the ground.

At this, those who heard began to go away one at a time, the older ones first, until only Jesus was left, with the woman still standing there. Jesus straightened up and asked her, "Woman, where are they? Has no one condemned you?"

"No one, sir," she said.

"Then neither do I condemn you," Jesus declared. "Go now and leave your life of sin."

John 8:3–11

The people who brought to Jesus the woman taken in adultery were right. According to the law, she should have been put to death.

Jesus showed by his actions that there are many times when mercy must take precedence over judgment. Jesus didn't see the woman as an adulteress. He saw her as a human being created in God's image. He saw her as someone worthy of redemption.

A friend of mine once told me that he often prayed, "Lord, help me to be constructive and not destructive in my relationships with others. Help me to enter into every situation with the intent to build up and not to tear down." I believe that's the attitude Christ had and it is demonstrated in his continual kindness toward many of those who were written off by proper society as worthless sinners who deserved no mercy.

Remember, Christians aren't perfect, just forgiven.

Goodness

Jesus' kindness was tempered with goodness.

Jesus entered the temple area and drove out all who were buying and selling there. He overturned the tables of the money changers and the benches of those selling doves. "It is written," he said to them, "'My house will be called a house of prayer,' but you are making it a 'den of robbers.'"

Matthew 21:12–13

Remember that goodness puts limits on kindness. There comes a time when you have to put your foot down and say, "This is wrong, and I won't put up with it."

It was St. Augustine who urged Christians with, "liberty in non-essentials, unity in essentials, and in all things, love." It's important to keep in mind that there are some essentials, some areas where kindness must give way to judgment. There are some times when mercy is not compatible with justice and justice takes precedence over mercy.

Jesus forgave the woman taken in adultery, although he commanded her not to return to her life of sin. On the other hand, there were some sins that were so grievous that Jesus had to say, This has to stop and it has to stop now. Jesus was kind but he did not confuse kindness with tolerance of improper behavior.

Faithfulness

Jesus was faithful unto death.

From that time on Jesus began to explain to his disciples that he must go to Jerusalem and suffer many things at the hands of the elders, chief priests and teachers of the law, and that he must be killed and on the third day be raised to life.

Peter took him aside and began to rebuke him. "Never, Lord!" he said. "This shall never happen to you!"

Jesus turned and said to Peter, "Get behind me, Satan! You are a stumbling block to me; you do not have in mind the things of God, but the things of men."

Matthew 16:21–23

Jesus knew that his calling was to go into Jerusalem, where he would be put to death on the cross. Naturally he was dreading it, as anyone would. But despite his natural dread and fear, he would not be dissuaded. He was determined to be faithful to the mission God had given him.

In this instance he drew his boundaries firmly. He could not be faithful to the task his Father had given him and faithful at the same time to Peter, who clearly did not want his Lord and friend to die.

Gentleness

Jesus was capable of great gentleness and tenderness.

> When Mary reached the place where Jesus was and saw him, she fell at his feet and said, "Lord, if you had been here, my brother would not have died."
> When Jesus saw her weeping, and the Jews who had come along with her also weeping, he was deeply moved in spirit and troubled. "Where have you laid him?" he asked.
> "Come and see, Lord," they replied.
> Jesus wept.
>
> John 11:32–35

> People were also bringing babies to Jesus to have him touch them. When the disciples saw this, they rebuked them. But Jesus called the children to him and said, "Let the little children come to me, and do not hinder them, for the kingdom of God belongs to such as these."
>
> Luke 18:15–16

I believe the depth of Jesus' gentleness can be seen in the two examples above. He openly wept in the presence of his friends. The Bible doesn't say exactly why he wept. It's doubtful that it was because Lazarus had died. After all, he knew that he was going to bring Lazarus back from the grave. I think it's more likely that he wept because his heart was touched by the grief of Lazarus's sisters—Mary and Martha—and their friends.

I don't know how you feel about it, but I admire a man who is strong enough, brave enough, and gentle enough to cry in public. That's just not an easy thing for many men to do. That's the way it is now, and I'm sure it was that way two thousand years ago.

Jesus had a gentle heart. And a gentle touch—so gentle that mothers brought their babies to him to receive his blessing. Jesus wasn't some politician, kissing babies for votes. He was a gentle, loving, caring man who truly loved children and wanted to bless them.

Remember, Jesus was tough and rugged when it was required. It took guts to confront the religious leaders of his day as he often did. It took a rugged individual to go into the temple and drive out the money changers. But because Jesus demonstrated all of the fruit of the Spirit in equal measure, he knew when to be gentle and when to be tough and confrontational.

Self-Control

Jesus exhibited great self-control.

Jesus, full of the Holy Spirit, returned from the Jordan and was led by the Spirit in the desert, where for forty days he was tempted by the devil. He ate nothing during those days, and at the end of them he was hungry.

The devil said to him, "If you are the Son of God, tell this stone to become bread."

Jesus answered, "It is written: 'Man does not live on bread alone.'"

The devil led him up to a high place and showed him in an instant all the kingdoms of the world. And he said to him, "I will give you all their authority and splendor, for it has been given to me, and I can give it to anyone I want to. So if you worship me, it will all be yours."

Jesus answered, "It is written: 'Worship the Lord your God and serve him only.'"

The devil led him to Jerusalem and had him stand on the highest point of the temple. "If you are the Son of God," he said, "throw yourself down from here. For it is written:

'He will command his angels concerning you
   to guard you carefully;
they will lift you up in their hands,
   so that you will not strike your foot against a stone.'"

Jesus answered, "It says: 'Do not put the Lord your God to the test.'"
Luke 4:1–12

It's impossible for us to understand exactly what was going on during the temptation of Christ. All we can know is that Jesus was seriously tempted, and he chose to walk away from it.

The same thing occurred when Jesus was arrested in the Garden of Gethsemane. Peter, still trying to keep Jesus from going to the cross, pulled out his sword and began to fight, but Jesus said:

Put your sword back in its place, . . . for all who draw the sword will die by the sword. Do you think I cannot call on my Father, and he will at once put at my disposal more than twelve legions of angels? But how then would the Scriptures be fulfilled that say it must happen in this way?
Matthew 26:52–54

Again, Jesus must have been seriously tempted to call on those angels and escape the cross but he wouldn't do it. He was a man of great self-control, just as he was a man of great love, joy, peace, patience, kindness, goodness, faithfulness, and gentleness.

We would all benefit tremendously from emulating Christ's wonderful example. What better system of morality is there?

Are you ready to live a life that bears the fruit of the Spirit? Yes, life in this world is often troubling and difficult, but with the help of God's Spirit, you can rise above it.

My prayer for you is that God will bless you as you seek to live the way he wants you to live. If enough of us seek to live this way, we truly can change the world!

Notes

Chapter 1   *Assume Moral Responsibility*

1. William J. Bennett, "Getting Used to Decadence: The Spirit of Democracy in Modern America," The Heritage Lectures, no. 477 (1993), as quoted in *American Values: Opposing View Points* (San Diego: Greenhaven Press, 1995), 107.

2. James A Baker III, "Values Lapse with a Price to Pay," *Washington Times*, 11 July 1994, A16.

3. Charles Colson and Jack Eckerd, "Why Has Hard Work Fallen on Hard Times?" *Christianity Today*, 10 February 1992, 34–37.

4. Bennett, "Getting Used to Decadence," 109.

5. Ibid.

6. Anthony Harrigan, *St. Croix Review*, June 1992.

7. Dwight D. Murphey, "American's Civilizational Crisis: The Rise of Internal Barbarism," *Conservative Review*, vol. 4, no. 5 (September/October 1993), 123–30.

Chapter 2   *Morality Comes from Inside Out*

1. Let me state my position on marriage. I don't believe that the Bible speaks out about how marriage is instituted, but it does make clear that marriage is something very important. There is a dangerous move in America to forgo the formality of a traditional marriage for a common-law marriage. I will never support or encourage this informal marriage arrangement because of the incredible risk involved in entering into a relationship that does not have the support of the state, church, and

197

family. Expecting this type of marriage to work well is like going to Las Vegas to make money. It can happen but it is *very* risky!

I support such organizations as Love Can Wait and Why Wait, which encourage young people to make a decision to wait for a traditional marriage relationship before engaging in sex.

2. Bennett, "Getting Used to Decadence," 112.

3. Kurt D. Bruner, *Responsible Living in an Age of Excuses* (Chicago: Moody Press, 1992), 162.

Chapter 3   *Step One: Love, the Foundation*

1. Alan Loy McGinnis, *The Power of Optimism* (San Francisco: Harper & Row, 1990), 113.

2. Judith C. Lechman, *The Spirituality of Gentleness* (San Francisco: Harper & Row, 1987), 168.

3. McGinnis, *The Power of Optimism*, 115–16.

4. John Perkins and Tom A. Tarrants, III, *He's My Brother* (Grand Rapids: Chosen, 1994).

Chapter 4   *Step Two: Joy*

1. McGinnis, *The Power of Optimism*, 92.

2. Daniel Goleman, *Emotional Intelligence* (New York: Bantam, 1995), 87–88.

3. McGinnis, *The Power of Optimism*, 100.

Chapter 5   *Step Three: Peace*

1. *State of the World's Children* (New York: United Nations Children's Fund, 1996).

2. C. S. Lewis, *Mere Christianity* (New York: Macmillan, 1943), 72.

Chapter 7   *Step Five: Kindness*

1. Khalil Gibran, *Sand and Foam: The Book of Aphorisms* (New York: A. A. Knopf, 1995), 56.

Chapter 8   *Step Six: Goodness*

1. Billy Graham, *The Holy Spirit* (Waco: Word, 1978), 200.

2. Charles Colson, "The Upside of Pessimism," *Christianity Today*, 15 August 1994, 64.

Chapter 9   *Step Seven: Faithfulness*

1. Ralph Kinney Bennett, "How Honest Are We?" *Reader's Digest*, December 1995, 49–55.

Chapter 10   *Step Eight: Gentleness*

1. Graham, *The Holy Spirit*, 207.
2. Raleigh Washington and Glen Kehrein, *Breaking Down Walls* (Chicago: Moody, 1993), 160.
3. Lechman, *The Spirituality of Gentleness*, 13.
4. David D. Burns, *The Feeling Good Handbook* (New York: Plume Books, 1990), 377.
5. Ibid., 386.
6. Lechman, *The Spirituality of Gentleness*, 142.
7. Ibid., 144–45.

Chapter 11   *Step Nine: Self-Control*

1. Graham, *The Holy Spirit*, 210.

Chapter 12   *Lessons from the Life of Christ*

1. Andrew Murray, *Abide in Christ* (New Canaan, Conn.: Keats Publishing, 1973), 127.

Dr. Robert A. Schuller is the vice chairman of the Crystal Cathedral Ministries, an international ministry with offices in Canada, Australia, South Africa, Moscow, and Amsterdam. The headquarters is in Garden Grove, California, on the Crystal Cathedral Campus where the *Hour of Power* is produced and aired around the world. Schuller frequently delivers the morning message on the broadcast.

Dr. Schuller is also the executive director of the Rancho Capistrano Spiritual Growth Center in San Juan Capistrano, California, which is home to the church he founded in 1981, a retreat center, and a school. He is the host of the syndicated daily radio program *Balanced for Life* and the author of several books, including the bestselling *Dump Your Hang-Ups . . . without Dumping Them on Others* and *What Happens to Good People When Bad Things Happen*.